CIVIL RENEWAL

Mending the Hole in the Social Ozone Layer

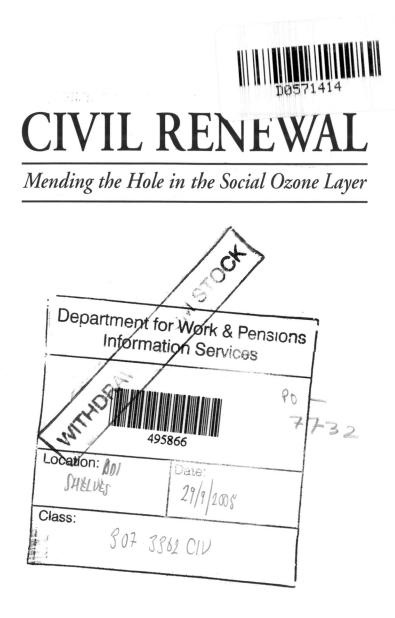

For Gill, Sophie, Jane & Balsall Heath

CIVIL RENEWAL

Mending the Hole in the Social Ozone Layer

Dr Dick Atkinson

BREWIN BOOKS

First published by
Brewin Books Ltd, 56 Alcester Road,
Studley, Warwickshire B80 7LG in 2004
www.brewinbooks.com

ISBN 1 85858 267 9

A Cataloguing in Publication Record
for this title is available from the British Library.

Typeset in Times
Printed in Great Britain by
The Cromwell Press

CONTENTS

PREFACE

A pen, they say, is mightier than the sword. But many is the time that I would have preferred a sword to cut a path through the tangled undergrowth of red- tape and inappropriate policies and practices so that the route to civil renewal in Balsall Heath and other neighbourhoods in the country could have been easier, less stressful and time-consuming.

However, now that something of a path has been hacked out in some neighbourhoods in the country, it is sensible to draw some conclusions and make some suggestions about how to do it again and again in many other neighbourhoods and in a less time-consuming manner. In the hope that others don't have to re-invent too much of the wheel, this book aims to show both practitioners and policy makers how to proceed in a spirit of partnership.

Yet, the path is not complete and the destination – the repairing of the hole in the social ozone layer – still some distance away. Whether we will get there has yet to be demonstrated. So, while I hope the book which follows makes it more likely that many will arrive at the end of the road, there is still work to be done before they can do so.

More people than I can mention have contributed to the experiences and ideas which follow. In Birmingham they include Gloria Dillion, Naseem Akhtar, Mohammed Mahboob, Raja Amin, Pat Wing, Abdul Hamid, Anita Halliday, Val Hart, Angus Kennedy, Ian Edwards, Neville Brown, Danny Bailey, Anne Molloy, Naeem Qureshi, Mohammed Shafique, Mohammed Amin, Tony Smith, Steve Botham, Steve Belling, Chris Wadhams & Roger Patrick.

In other regions they include Sylvana Mansell, Barry Schofield, Helen Whitney, Keith Proctor & Stephen Thake.

Nationally, they include Helen Edwards, David Blunkett, Johnathan Sacks, Peter Lambert, Neville Simms, Henry Tam, David Willets, Oliver Letwin & Paddy Ashdown.

All have contributed to the ideas and suggestions contained in this book. The best of these are theirs. The errors and false trails which remain are mine. But, I do hope that the best overwhelms the worst and that this book acts as both the pen and the sword for the many Naseems, Glorias, Sylvanas, Helens, Alisons, Hamids, Carries and Pats of this world. For, in their hands lies the success of the next generation. Can we put back into their future more than we have taken out in recent times?

Lastly, but by no means least, I am deeply grateful to Rozie Gayle who has typed and re-typed this book more times than she cares to remember. Without her, it would remain an unreadable mess. Rozie, you are a star.

EXECUTIVE SUMMARY
OF RECOMMENDATIONS

Chapter 1:
Renewing the 3,000 excluded neighbourhoods which disfigure the nation has, so far, proved too difficult despite many costly top down initiatives by successive Governments. So, ways must be found of making it far easier and more straightforward for Active Citizens to build strong, sustainable, communities in the neighbourhoods where they live.

Chapter 2:
Before it can be made easier for ordinary people to build solutions which both work and last, it must be recognised that the problem which residents face in excluded neighbourhoods is not so much material as social and cultural deprivation and poverty of the spirit.

There is a hole in the social ozone layer and we need to demonstrate this to politicians, policy makes and statutory professionals.

Chapter 3:
It will be difficult, but it is essential, to help these key players to understand that they and the Welfare State which was constructed during the twentieth century have become part of the problem.

To arrive at a solution, we need a national conversation which helps to change the culture and the way we think about how to care for each other.

Chapter 4:
In place of consulting a very few residents, an array of active citizens need to be empowered to build social capital, create local associations, both scrutinise local services and, where appropriate, manage the delivery of these.

While many will do this voluntarily, each neighbourhood's volunteers need at least one employed Capacity Builder who will identify, support, and assist with their training and provide them with resources.

It is possible for Statutory Agencies to put a price on the work of Active Citizens and Capacity Builders. For, their job is made easier and more effective if their services are well received by a responsive community. So, the funds for the building of Civil Renewal should come not from external grants but from the mainstream budgets of statutory players.

It is possible for LSP's to act as an 'inspectorate' of neighbourhoods (Ofsthood) and to audit the quality of life in those neighbourhoods which fall within their boundaries. The worst neighbourhoods should be put in special measures as a signal of intent that LSP's and HMG are determined to succeed and will not accept the poor quality of life in the most difficult neighbourhoods.

Chapter 5:
In addition to a Capacity Builder, each neighbourhood also needs:

* A Neighbourhood Manager
* A Neighbourhood Strategic Partnership (NSP)
* A Neighbourhood Development Plan
* A Neighbourhood Budget gained by assembling, disassembling and reassembling Mainstream Budgets.

Active Citizens and Strong Neighbourhoods imply the need for Statutory partners to move from 'doing' to 'enabling'. This entails the devolution to neighbourhoods of all services that can be delivered locally. Some of these will be delivered by NSPs, some by residents themselves.

The change in role for Statutory Partners and Local Authorities is dramatic and will entail persuasion, training and resources. Best practice will require rewards and poor practice sanctions.

Chapter 6:
Hitherto, only a few of the nation's 3,000 excluded neighbourhoods have recovered and costly renewal initiatives have failed.

Thus, in place of top-down externally funded renewal initiatives, a series of bottom up programmes are needed in which the strong help the week and which are funded from mainstream budgets.

If all 3,000 are to be included, a series of Regional Rolling Programmes of Neighbourhood Renewal is required which is lead by the few advanced or guide neighbourhoods and experienced resident consultants.

These programmes should be actively backed by Central, Local Government and LSP's.

Chapter 7:
The involvement of many Active Citizens in the Civil Renewal of their neighbourhoods is called Participatory Democracy. This needs to work in partnership with and breath fresh life into Representative Democracy. This will change the role of the local Councillor, requires Local Authorities to develop a more strategic role and

should result in closing the gap between the people and their representatives. In turn, this should result in increased numbers of people voting in local elections.

Chapter 8:
Active Citizens, Strong Neighbourhoods and the effective Management of Neighbourhoods can't be sustained without the development of common standards, values and respected, authoritative, role models.

Neither Civil Renewal nor the development of a respected local authority will grow quickly. Filling the hole in the Social Ozone Layer will take at least a generation.

Chapter 9:
Local Civil Renewal and local figures of authority need the clear and unequivocal support of national leaders in all Political Parties, as well as faith and other leaders.

All aged 18 plus should be encouraged to undertake a year of community service. This could be rewarded by a 50% reduction in student fees or by a weekly communal wage for those who do not go to college.

Graduation might coincide with a Nationally recognised Day of Duty which symbolises the fact that all must put back into society more than they take out.

As well as a series of Regional Rolling Programmes of recovery we need a series of regional debates leading into a national one about how to renew society and develop a new compact between the individual, the third sector and the public sector of the state.

This debate should be lead not just by party leaders but by faith and other leaders as we strive for a new social consensus.

Chapter 10:
Neighbourhoods can't be renewed and, the hole in the social ozone layer can't be filled, unless we devise new policies and programmes in place of those derived from traditional Socialist and Conservative modes of thinking.

New solutions require holistic ways of thinking about the interests of society as a whole, not partial ones derived from ideas formed from different parts of the class divided industrial society of the last century. Filling the hole in the social ozone layer requires a new kind of politics and new way of thinking about society and the role of the individual within it.

In effect, successful Civil Renewal entails replacing the Welfare State with a Welfare Society and devising a new compact between the individual and the state.

"Love your neighbours as yourself"

The Bible

"The whole field of security .....once the domain of voluntary mutual aid, (might become) divided between the state and private business conducted for gain"

William Beveridge

"If you do not steward the earth and put more back into it than you take out of it, the soil will turn to sand and you will starve"

Elementary principle of farming

Chapter One

INTRODUCTION AND CONTEXT

A long time ago when I left the London School of Economics some of my friends and colleagues expected me to 'go into politics' to try to make the world a better place from the Top-down, via a life in Whitehall and, maybe, the cabinet. However, 34 years ago I was invited to live in Birmingham's inner ring area of Balsall Heath and try to make a difference there from the Bottom-up.

My experience from the Bottom-up in Balsall Heath has been that regardless of the party they belong to, well intentioned politicians will not get their Top-down policies right when they derive them from remote political theories of left or right about how people and society are supposed to behave. They need to listen hard to what real people from the Bottom-up actually say is needed and frame policies according to the practical experience of 'what works'. After a long period of being prevented from listening because their partial party political view of the world made them deaf to ordinary voices, some politicians at the Top are at last coming into productive alignment with those of us at the Bottom. Some are jettisoning ideology and letting the light of reality and common sense illuminate their thinking. But, there is a distance yet to go. This book sets out to travel that distance.

Thirty-four years ago in 1970, Balsall Heath was a bleak, desolate and troubled place. Its native white working class population was being broken up by the end of the manufacturing era and by planners who moved many residents from their 100 years old houses to new municipal tower blocks which they built in Birmingham's outer ring estates. Newcomers from Idi Amin's Uganda, the Indian Sub-continent, other parts of Africa, the Caribbean and China were moving in as nowhere else would have them.

Thus, the once cohesive and stable 100-year-old white working class community was replaced by a fractured, lonely and atomised one which came from the 4 corners of the world. Once strong, the neighbourhood was now weak. Crime and prostitution had once been largely confined to three roads. It now spread rapidly, in part as a result of Roy Jenkins' Liberal reforms, in part, because residents did not know how to resist it. By 1980 some 450 prostitutes, controlled by 40 pimps, dominated the corners of most roads where 15,000 people now lived. Of these, 60% were of Eastern origin, 20% African Caribbean and 20% white. The pimps hooked vulnerable young women onto drugs, then forced them to go onto the street to earn their next fix. The money the pimps made from the prostitutes was used to drive a major, multi-million pound, drugs industry. They owned BMW's, wore expensive jewellery and were a menacing presence. They had become the new role models for young, vulnerable, boys and girls.

Residents lived in their back rooms, for a light in the front room would attract the door knock and abuse of a kerb-crawler. Neither women nor men would venture out at night or into parks by day. Children did not play outside.

Health, including mental health was poor. Educational standards were low. The two local secondary schools closed, one because parents chose to send their children to schools in leafier suburbs, the other because the Council did not like its Grammar School ethos. The adult unemployment figure reached 38%. The ratio of those voting in local elections fell to just 2 out of 10.

Memories from those times are seared into the author's memory. They include:

* Being shown, by fifteen year old Kevin the vandalized empty house next door to where he lived. Its roof and floorboards were missing, thus exposing joists and beams. His father had hung himself from one of these. He pointed to it and wept.

* Seeing in the cold light of day the ground floor steel-mesh reinforced but shattered windows in a block of flats. The night before, a client who had short changed a drug dealer had been stripped naked and run headfirst through the window. Left hanging half in and half out of the window, his blood still lay on the floor. His squeals of pain and fright had caused residents in the rest of the block to bolt their doors, turn off their lights and live another night in fear and torment.

* This tower block marked the rear entrance to the local police station. Police drove their cars in and out of it with their eyes fixed straight ahead, for they supposed there was nothing they could do. Residents felt abandoned. The few private houses were put up for sale. But nobody wanted to buy them.

* Listening to Gloria, a young mother of three, explain that she had to move as she feared for her children's safety and dare not let them play even in front of her house. She had put her house on the market 3 months before at £20k. She had not received one offer. It stayed on the market for a year. She reduced the price to £5k, but still no offer was received. It was valueless. She was distressed.

* The Cannon Hill Pub had once been used to accommodate visiting teams to the nearby Edgbaston Cricket ground. It had become a place to fear, it specialised in drugs and items which had 'fallen off the back of a lorry.' In the centre of a densely populated part of Balsall Heath, residents would run by it in daylight and walk half a mile out of their way at night to avoid having to pass it.

- Having a discussion with a local Councillor and the area's then M.P., Roy Hattersley, in which they defended themselves for not being seen as useful by local people. They explained that they were working to improve local circumstances by redistributing the taxpayer's money in the Town Hall and Whitehall. They told me not to worry and to leave the improvement of the area to them. "We are the politicians, not you," they said. "Trust us."

- Having a discussion with a liberally minded lecturer who lived in an affluent suburb. He explained to me that local people who objected to prostitution were 'militant Muslims' and 'authoritarian fascists' because prostitutes were 'only body workers trying to earn an honest penny who had been driven to it by Margaret Thatcher.'

- Listening to a very senior police officer tell residents who were begging for action to 'clean and green their area and make it safe' that this was not possible as they did not have enough resources. Thus, if residents did not like living in Balsall Heath, they should, he said: "Move to a place they liked".

So, for the last 34 years I've worked with residents and anyone who would listen to change these bleak times into better ones. It has not been easy. Indeed, it has been very difficult. In part, the story this book tells is about how success was won and how it can be made easier not just in Balsall Heath, but also in the 3,000 plus similar inner and outer city neighbourhoods which disgrace the nation. Today, Balsall Heath can boast about these facts:

- Street Corner Prostitution is long gone, as is much attendant crime and nuisance.

- The Cannon Hill Pub is now a Training Centre.

- House prices are rising faster than anywhere else in Birmingham. Gloria's house which was worthless sold the other day for £125,000.

- Last year Balsall Heath came runner up in the urban section of the national Britain in Bloom competition.

- Balsall Heath has a village or Neighbourhood Forum which enables residents to deliver some home grown services and scrutinise statutory ones to ensure they are top notch.

- In 2002, only 6% of people in 37 of the City's 39 wards said their quality of life was improving. In one other, Castle Vale, which is a HAT, 33% said it was improving. In Balsall Heath the statistic was 66%.

- Residents from elsewhere in the country and policy makers now flock to Balsall Heath and ask: "Can you show us how you did this? We want to follow suit".

These statistics of recovery can be brought to life with the help of some newer, pleasanter, memories:

- I was walking down a street with my friend Raja Amin. Raja is a Trades Unionist and resident. He had applied the organising tactics familiar to him at work to the streets where he lived. He had placed 30 groups each made up of 6 residents on the streets most affected by the kerb crawlers. They wrote down their registration numbers and shamed them away. Once the demand had gone, the supply faded and left.

    Suddenly, a young white mother with two children at her side threw her arms round Raja, kissed him on the check and said "Thank you." We asked her "What for?" She said: "I'm wearing lipstick and a skirt for the first time and I've lived here for 20 years. I feel free."

- The look on Gloria's face when she told me that she had again put her house up for sale ten years later and, within the week, it had gone for £125k.

    The only reason she wanted to move now was because she had become employed as a local development worker and residents in need of advice were knocking on her door from 6.00am through to 11pm. Ten years ago she had wanted to move because of fear but could not. Now she wanted to move because of the success of her efforts and could do so.

- Louise, a volunteer at the Forum's Tree Nursery saying: "After coming here I've slept soundly for the first time for years."

- Hamid, a Muslim and one of our Neighbourhood Wardens, saw a can being thrown into the gutter by two young men of African origin who were changing the oil in their car on the high street at midnight. "I think you've dropped this", he said. "Pick it up." They questioned his parentage, threatened to hit him and asked what business of his it was. He told them and said the area was now different and that we were all looking after it. After a heated exchange, one of the Africans said grudgingly. "O.k., I'll pick it up if you say please." Hamid said "Sir, I'd be grateful if you'd pick up the can and put it in a bin. Would you, please." The man did so and said: "Sorry, I live in Handsworth. I don't suppose you'd come over there and help us out, would you, please."

- On hearing we had come runners up in the Britain in Bloom competition a shopkeeper saying: "Fancy us, Balsall Heath! Everyone had written us off, but we've made it. Its fantastic. If we can do this, we can do anything."

Many of the white people who were re-housed from the 'slums' of Balsall Heath went to live in the municipal estate of Kings Norton. In 1999 it became a New Deal for Community area (NDC) with £50m to spend but with no resident involvement although NDC rules insisted upon this.

- Residents in culturally mixed Balsall Heath were invited to go to outer-ring Kings Norton to show how to get residents involved. They were frightened. "That's BNP territory. We'll get attacked," they said. But, they also acknowledged that they now lived in the place which had once been home to those who now lived in Kings Norton. The new Balsall Heathans felt an obligation to help if they could. So, they went, identified some particular jobs which needed doing, including clearing the rubbish dumped in a potentially attractive stream which ran right through the estate.

- Before long, the white residents of Kings Norton were bringing tea and biscuits to the residents of Balsall Heath. "Are you Council?" they asked. When they learned the truth they said "Will you come and work for us permanently?" The Balsall Heathans refused and said: "But, we'll show you how to do it. We'll do it with you for a bit, then you take over." They shook hands and embraced each other.

After the efforts of very many people and the passage of 34 years, the neighbourhood of Balsall Heath is en-route to sustainable recovery and those of us who are getting on in years can think of passing the work on to others who can now manage without us.

But, it has been a painful and very difficult uphill struggle. Many is the time when the gradient of the climb seemed too steep and we feared we would slip back and not make it to the top of the hill.

The Town Hall and Whitehall could have levelled the ground so that progress was easier. But, inadvertently, perhaps because they feared a strong neighbourhood, they made the climb seem almost vertical. I have to report that I and my friends elsewhere who are engaged on the renewal of their area have made progress despite, not because of, 'the system'. Too often it was an obstacle which steepened the slope and did not level it.

The ideological blockage in the mind of the partisan politician and those who will not 'listen' but can only 'tell' can be illustrated by these stories:

- After the two secondary schools closed, one quite literally because it was too good, one because it was too bad, some local children did not catch the bus to the out of town school, but played truant and made life for adults a nuisance. So, we created a small secondary school for them with the help of their worried parents. It was an independent charity with the same legal status as Eton and Harrow. It became a success. The truants attended and gained respectable GCSE results.

  The then Leader of Birmingham Council visited and said: " I can see it's a success. But, as it's so good, why are you doing this privately? Shouldn't we be doing it publicly? You should hand it to us." The answer was, of course, that had it been left to the Council it wouldn't have existed. And, if they took it over, it would lose the sense of local ownership and fail.

- Houses to either side of a main shopping road were knocked down in a 'slum clearance programme and the well intentioned Council decided to build a new primary school and small park where they had stood. The shopkeepers complained, saying they needed houses to be built as they were losing customers and facing bankruptcy. The existing primary schools said their rolls would fall further as a result of a new school. They too wanted houses to be built. And, so did the residents. None the less, the Council went ahead and built a new school and park. It called the school Nelson Mandela.

  Desmond Tutu was visiting the country and the Council invited him to open the school as Nelson Mandela was still in prison. Residents pointed out that this would be a good excuse for a celebratory party in the park at which Desmond Tutu could speak. The council said: "This is too dangerous. We can't expose this VIP to the dangers of being at a public gathering in Balsall Heath."

  Residents persisted. They reminded the Council about what conditions were like in South Africa and that this was Balsall Heath. "Exactly", said the Council spokesman. " Maybe if residents gathered outside the school, Desmond Tutu could wave at them from inside it, protected by specially reinforced glass."

  Residents felt insulted, phoned the Bishop's Palace in Johannesburg, and invited him to their party in the park. He agreed. Some 3,000 residents danced attendance with him. He said: "You are a rainbow people. I just hope that one day I can see in my own homeland the same pride that I see in your eyes and the song in your heart. You are an inspiration to me…" The residents were ecstatic.

- My neighbours, Tony and Mrs Judith Stokes wished to stay in the terraced house they owned. But the Council had compulsorily purchased and knocked down the dozen houses which had butted on to theirs to turn into a 'mini park'.

  Tony and Judith said: "Don't knock us down too. We want to stay." The officials said: "But we've just knocked down the terraced house next to yours and its adjoining wall. So, your wall is now only one brick thick and that's illegal and unsafe. We will have to knock you down."

Tony and Judith said: "But, if we build the second set of bricks back up, we'll be safe. So, as a brick is 4½ inches wide, please sell us a strip that wide of your land and we'll build at our own cost."

"Can't do that," said the Council officials. "We can only sell land by the metre and we can't sell it just the length of your house, we have to sell it the length of the house and garden."

"You win," said Tony and Judith, "We'll borrow the money by mortgaging our house and we'll buy it and build the wall." They did.

The irony is that the Council then failed to maintain the little park they had built. So, Tony and Judith litter pick it and plant it with bulbs and flowers. It became a 'confused', un-owned, space in the hands of the Council, then owned again because of Tony and Judith who now care for it.

The gulf between the street and the Council Chamber, the voter and the politician yawned wide and deep in those days. Any resident in any inner and outer city neighbourhood has a series of similar stories to tell. It really is little wonder that as few as 2 out of 10 people now wield the vote which the suffragettes and others won 100 years ago. Since those heady days, representative democracy really has hit hard times and is in serious danger of becoming irreparably damaged to the point where extremist parties can cash in and, quite literally, make a killing.

At such times as these stories occurred, it was tempting to give up and slide back down to the bottom of the hill. But, I was buoyed up by three things. First, my family. Second, the fact that there were a few others undergoing a similar experience in other parts of the country. Angus Kennedy in Castle Vale, Steve Stride in Popular Harca, Andrew Mawson in Bromley by Bow, Barry Schofield in Bradford, Gerard Murden in Toxteth and others have achieved wonders in their neighbourhoods. There aren't many such people in the country, perhaps 20 or 30 in all. But we did and do have a very common experience. Third, the ambition to make it easier for others who would, one day, set out on the task to improve the 3,000 excluded neighbourhoods which are to be found scattered in the inner and outer rings of every urban area of the land. The point is so important that it deserves emphasis.

People often tell me that I have helped to make the difference in Balsall Heath and that I and my friends in the 20+ other successfully renewing neighbourhoods elsewhere are, in some way, special, even unique. They mean this as a complement, but add: "So, you see, it can't be done in the 3,000 other excluded neighbourhoods of the land, because there are not 3,000 of you. You are too exceptional."

This is a flattering, but serious, error. Before Roger Bannister first ran the mile in under 4 minutes everyone said it wasn't possible. Then, after he achieved it, they said it couldn't be done again as he had freak and over sized lungs. Yet, today, everyone does it.

Angus, Steve, Andrew, Barry and I, are merely at the Roger Bannister stage of the renewal race. And, 3,000 others can be found swiftly, especially if the track is levelled and the boulders, crevasses and other obstacles of red-tape and officialdom are removed. Instead of the runners being harassed and hounded by 'the system' at every curve of the track, they should be cheered on and resourced by it.

This book aims to level the playing field and enable the Bottom and the Top to work in productive harmony so that all 3000 neighbourhoods can be helped by 3,000 ordinary mortals.

To do that, we will have to radically transform:

- The capacity of people who live in neighbourhoods to control and shape their destiny.
- The Town Halls of the land, the way services are delivered to residents in neighbourhoods and the way residents are resourced.
- Whitehall and the way it devises and delivers renewal initiatives, for, up to now, most have failed to make much difference.
- The way politicians think and feel about helping people in despairing inner and outer city neighbourhoods.
- The number of people who vote.
- The way the whole country thinks about the way people can most effectively care for and support each other.

An almost impossible challenge? But, one to which we have to rise. A variety of London based Think Tanks began to explore the theoretical and policy implications of this challenge in the 1980's and 90's – DEMOS, IPPR, the IEA. Politicians such as Tony Blair, David Blunkett, Oliver Letwin, Paddy Ashdown and David Willetts accepted the need for the centre ground of political thinking to move.

Bill Clinton spoke of Triangulation in the 1990's. By this he meant that the wise politician would take neither a partial left wing working class approach nor a partial right wing affluent one, but would rise above both of these and take an over-view which included the best of both views and ' triangulate' them into an all- encompassing view.

Tony Blair speaks of the 'Third way.' This has been sadly misunderstood and derided by many commentators. But it has much merit. The Third way suggests that the Conservative's first way and old Labour's second way are both one sided views of society-wide needs. The secret of successful renewal and progress is to blend them together into a Third way which makes sense to ordinary, non party political, folk – and works because it connects with both sides of the coin of reality.

The Third way is not a compromise between the extremes of left and right or available only to New Labour. It aims to include the third force of active citizens in the management of their own lives in the neighbourhoods where they live and raise their families. It is this powerful alliance of citizens, the enabling state and the market that defines the basis of the third way. This is available to all the parties – if only they can recognise the practical merit of it.

The principles behind this way and the reforms it implies are explored in this book and these chapters:

Chapter 2:
Considers the extent to which life in communities in the neighbourhoods where people live has become fractured and unsupportive. It is argued that social capital has been frittered and that there is a hole in the social ozone layer.

Chapter 3:
Looks at the causes of the hole in the ozone layer, the pace of technological change, post enlightenment ideas which have replaced enduring values with relativity and reason, and the Welfare State.

Chapter 4:
Examines how unconfident people in excluded neighbourhoods can build their capacity to make things happen. In every neighbourhood there are some people who can become the active agents of civil renewal.

Chapter 5:
Shows that active citizens need strong neighbourhoods. But, strong neighbourhoods can't develop unless they are managed differently. Each neighbourhood needs a neighbourhood manager, a joined up team of service deliverers and a budget – not new money, but existing mainstream money, which is used differently.

Chapter 6:
Describes how a rolling programme of civil renewal in neighbourhoods can be started in every urban area leading to the inclusion of all 3000 excluded ones.

Chapter 7:
Explains that confident people in strong neighbourhoods are practising Participatory Democracy and that this can help to restore faith in the Representative kind.

Chapter 8:
Shows how a cohesive authority can be asserted at neighbourhood level which binds people together.

Chapter 9:

Shows how local authority can be supported by national action and leadership. It explains why a national and series of regional debates about the hole in the social ozone layer are needed.

Chapter 10:

Examines the difficulty which ideologies of the left and right face in addressing civil renewal and shows how both need to change if they are to catch up with the needs and wishes of ordinary people.

Chapter 11:

Sums up the case and challenges local people and national leaders to join together to renew civil society and mend the hole in the social ozone layer.

Chapter Two

THE PROBLEM OUTLINED

Socialisation and Civilisation:

It is always tempting to live for today and to ignore the consequences of today's acts upon tomorrow's existence. Because the experience of life is so immediate for each individual, it is easy for us to forget that it is part of a never ending, steadily evolving, process in which we are each "But a grain of sand on the beach of time."

Each of us is most impressed with what is happening to us and what we are doing and feeling this day, this hour, this moment and how we respond to it in the next moment. In fact, we are witnessing just one tiny fragment of what is, in fact, a far wider, difficult to grasp, ever changing, social universe.

We can each begin to grasp the point in our own lives if we reflect not just on who we are now, but what we were like as an infant, teenager, young man or woman and what we have become since then and are evolving towards and what, when we are long gone, our children and children's children will inherit and transform.

If we now accept that we are all but one of very many people and that the age we live in is but one in a sequence of many, which both reaches back into the distant past and is also the springboard from which we will leap into the future, then we are quite literally "put in our place," humbled and given pause for thought. In this sense, whilst each of we are, of course, a unique individual, we are also an integral part of a far wider collectively with a common history and a future which will, at least in part, emerge from that history.

We can, of course, see and touch our cumulative physical creations, buildings, cities and so on, though we need the study of archaeology to tell us about the foundations of the previous buildings upon which they now stand and, indeed, why they are to be found at this particular location. It is not so easy to see our social creations. We can see people, but not the relations between them or the cultural foundations and experiences upon which they stand. However, it is worth, for a moment, imagining that we can. For, society, civilization, our collective history and current experience is not unlike a Cathedral, towering above us and standing four square around us.

Look down at your feet. You see only this or that flagstone and part of a pew. Look up and to your right and you see the vaulting South Wing, which houses the sculptures of Saints and Kings and the rainbow-like beauty of stained glass windows, separated by Norman arches and gargoyles. Look behind and you see the font and the bell ropes leading up to the Western tower which was partly destroyed by fire just 100 years ago, then rebuilt to suit modern taste. The scaffolding is still in place as the lighting is changed and electric lights replace the candelabras.

Over to the East are the carved chairs upon which a succession of Priests and Bishops have sat and, beyond them, the arched windows, which burst into another chrysanthemum shape of stained glass depicting scenes from the Old and New testament. Down the circular stone steps which lead to the crypt, the preserved beams and huge stone pillars stand on the foundations upon which the first church was constructed a thousand years ago.

It's difficult to see the whole unless we go outside and view it from a distance. This makes it easier to remember the context of the particular slab and pew and recognise their significance. For, without the whole, they are meaningless reminders of the value of this question and the two different answers to it: A passer by asks two workmen who seem to be laying stones one on the other this question: "What are you doing?"

The first man says: "Laying stones." The second says: "Building a Cathedral."

Our society and the civilization on which it stands is a social cathedral. Each generation and set of individuals have both preserved what exists and added stones to it and a window here, a new roof there. It has evolved and is evolving still – or is it? For, surely, nobody would willingly deny the next generation its inheritance of a social cathedral. It couldn't be, could it, that we have so failed to tend the fabric of the Cathedral that it crumbles and could fall, that the next generation will not inherit a Cathedral but a pile of stones, which give them no history, no identity, no future?

Socialisation

How is the social cathedral of civilization passed on from parent to child, from generation to generation, so that it develops and the child benefits from the accumulated edifice of past experience? Sociologists have a term to describe the process which takes place every time each new child is gradually weaned into breathing the social life of its peers and parents. They call it 'socialization', the way the child acquires and inherits its social genes from the particular cathedral, or mosque, or temple into which it is born and which guide it to act in ways congruent with those around it.

Every society we have known undertakes this process and most people in each society have a vitally important part to play in it, as follows:

Parents and relatives

Someone once said: "Give me the boy until he is seven years of age and I will give you the man." This means, of course, that the earliest formative influences on a child set them up – for good or ill – in later life and provide them with the coat peg of character upon which their more mature clothes of adult disposition will hang.

Another person said: "That mother has been really good at civilizing her boy's wilder passions." By this, she meant that her boy's more chaotic impulses, which could have damaged himself and others had been brought under control. In place of the weakness of indulgence, tough love had been practiced over a prolonged period. The person added: "Of course, she had the support of her partner and her mum (the boy's grandma) lived in the next street."

While the single parent can also 'civilize' her child, it is so much easier if there are two pairs of guiding hands and boys especially have a good male adult role model as well as a female one. Easier too, if there is the odd aunty and uncle on hand, let alone grandparents and good neighbours.

Another saying has it: The family is the cradle of civilization. Rabbi Neusener taught us that: 'Civilisation hangs suspended, from generation to generation, by the gossamer strand of memory. If only one cohort of mothers and fathers fails to convey to its children what it has learned from its parents, then the great chain of learning and wisdom snaps. If the guardians of human knowledge stumble only one time, in their fall collapses the whole edifice of knowledge and understanding.'

School

The importance of schooling for the socialisation of the child is second only to that of parents. Henry Morris, the inspirational Chief Education Officer, reminded us that the best school 'lies athwart its community' of families. It is not just 'in' the neighbourhood but a part 'of' it. It stands alongside and in place of parents. It extends and develops the character they laid down and opens the child's eyes to the wider world of accumulated experience and civilized awareness. The very best school does not just teach it. It lives it in the way it is organised. It teaches through doing as well as via the blackboard.

In this sense, education is crucially not just about creating an avenue to work. It is not about the economy alone. It is also about creating an avenue for life which leads from the past through the present and into the future. It is about the transition and inheritance of civilization and the development of it.

The Faith Establishment

Each world religion takes the messages we receive at home and school and extends them into a story about the point and purpose of life. It houses the social cathedral within the physical Cathedral and reaches beyond it to everyone's heart and mind at times of joy and sadness.

Each religion and the community which worships together brings order and stability in an otherwise rapidly changing and puzzling world. It even marks the different stages in our life with a series of rites of passage which condense the code of civilisation into a series of communal symbolic ceremonies.

Duties and Right of Passage

It is not easy to get parenting right. Parents, schools and faith groups, can all fail in their duty to steward civilization by not supporting the child adequately.

Because it is hard, takes self-sacrifice and moral courage, every known civilization evolved rites of passage, which lighten the burden and remind its citizens of their obligations. Rites of passage do this in symbolic, shorthand codes, which capture and convey tradition. They include:

- Recognising the birth of the child, naming and registering it and passing to it sacred mementoes.
- Giving it 'god-parents' should its parents fail or need support.
- Inducting it into the faith of its parents.
- Passing tests at school, gaining certificates and, quite literally, graduating and being inducted into fellowship of scholars.
- Gaining the key to the door and confirming the knowing youth into the faith they were given in their unknowing childhood.
- Engagement.
- Marriage.
- Birth and the cycle begin again except now the child-as-parent initiates their own child.
- Death, burial, the memory of and respect for the dead.

Civilisation and the Rites of Passage evolve over time as the experience of each new generation is added to the cathedral of the past. "It is written. But I say unto you ......" No civilisation has been able to do without them. Anyone who tries to do so dices with the death of civilisation and, thus, with our failure to show the next generation how to live in caring harmony with one another.

The neighbourhood or village

There is a wise African saying which tells us that "it takes a whole village to educate a child." In this country, each Town or City is made up of many urban villages or neighbourhoods. The way the influence of family, school, faith and rites of passage `is complemented by the village – or otherwise – is of crucial importance for the developing child. Are the lessons of home and school reinforced and extended by a positive neighbouring environment or contradicted and undermined?

Finally, come the wider Town and Nation. Is it at ease with itself? Is it harmonious and purposeful or mean and torn? Again, as the child moves into youthful maturity and adulthood, a positive wider society is the vital overarching piece of the jigsaw puzzle of their socialization and civilization.

Does it bolster their ability to steward the social terrain, extend their inheritance of civilization and enable them, in their turn, to teach to their children what they learned from those children's grandparent's?

Determination versus choice

Influenced by the economic determination of Karl Marx and the exactness of the physical sciences, some of the early sociologists took the notion of socialisation too far. They used it to show how everything the developing child did fitted into a pre-determined pattern of things. They described how an internalised set of attitudes and characteristics connected with a set of external expectations which meant the individual was the trapped and predictable plaything of a 'social system' which prescribed what action might be taken at any given time, thus leaving no room for what we understand as freedom or choice.

In so doing, they perhaps over-reacted against a pre-sociological view which held that the individual was free to do whatever they wanted, the only limit being the breadth of a person's imagination. Reality, surely, is to be found somewhere between these two views.

Even the simplest soul who has struggled to raise their children – rather than sat in the philosopher's or sociologist's chair in the Ivory Tower – can remind us that, even at a tender age, every child bristles with a powerful will. While key manifestations of that will echo and mimic the parent's smiles, frowns and kindnesses, every child tries to alter their environment to fit their advantage and satisfy their appetites, whether for food or love. As they grow up, they acquire ever more sophisticated and socially recognisable words and mannerisms to achieve their end and, in so doing, alter reality in no small part. Thus, does the cathedral evolve.

That is, while the child 'inherits' or 'acquires' speech, a language, from its parents and, eventually, the accumulated knowledge of much of the community, they do not simply mirror it. They also make it their own and, in so doing, push forward the frontiers of that knowledge. Whilst the determination or prescriptions of social inheritance mingles with and constrains 'free will' and 'choice' it does not prevent it. Merely, it predisposed it in one or more of a limited number of directions.

It simply isn't possible for the child to act outside of the evolving social cathedral unless, that is, it crumbles. Then the child and adult are lost. Worse, the thread upon which civilisation is suspended snaps. The child falls.

The physical environment

For centuries, the best farmers have known how to tend the earth they dig. They rotated crops, applied animal manure, left fields fallow. They put back into the earth more than they took out of it. They cleared the wilderness and made it more fertile and fruitful. They cared for and stewarded the earth.

This takes effort. It also takes thought, love, self-control and far-sightedness. For, it entails considering not just short-term individual gain for today but long-term mutual gain for tomorrow and the well-being of the next generation. Central to good stewarding is the ability to forsake the immediate gain of the moment, rise above and beyond the situation of today and take the long-view.

We have not all been like that. In the early 1900's, farmers in the American Mid-West created dust bowls and deserts out of fertile land by over-cropping for excessive immediate commercial gain. The Saharan desert remorselessly expands as more is taken out on the edges of it than is put back in. The rain forests shrink as timber is felled at an increasing rate in Latin America. In these cases, the farmers appeared to gain materially in the short run. But, they lost over the long term – and lost heavily. So have their children who, instead of inheriting a fertile earth, gained only barren land. Indeed, the history of the human race is littered with the skeletons of tribes and civilisations which cut off their nose to spite their face as they killed too many trees or over cropped the soil upon which their future existence depended.

Being a good steward is a hard lesson to learn. Perhaps that is why we are still not too good at it.

The dusty coal and other mines of medieval times appeared to leave little trace on the landscape and had little effect on the balance of nature. But, scientific and technological advances in the last two hundred years have increasingly changed all that. Many parts of the earth have been remorselessly scoured for coal and oil which has then been burned in furnaces, cars and planes. The rivers, sea and atmosphere have become polluted by toxic emissions. We have taken out much and put very little back.

There is now a hole in the ozone layer which has resulted in global warming. Thus, the ice at the North and South poles melts. When the environmentalists first told us about this 30 years ago, we did not hear or heed what they were worrying about. Then, their concern was expressed in the wings of the world theatre. Now, their story is told on the centre of the world stage.

People and their leaders have become so concerned that they now organise World Summits in Rio in 1992 and Johannesburg in 2002 to consider how the balance can be restored and how short term interests can be tempered within the context of longer term ones. This is still not proving to be easy. For, as with some farmers, powerful commercial interests are tempted to put short term gain first and put off all thought of tomorrow. But, the long-term interests of us all are already adversely affected.

However, at last, the debate has been joined up and most people can now see the need to tend and steward the green and physical environment in just the way the best farmer does. The debate, if not yet the implementation of its conclusion, has been won.

From the physical to the social environment

There is a now a similar debate to be staged about our social environment, the state of the social terrain we inhabit, the maintenance of the Cathedral of civilisation. Every new generation has a tendency to grumble about changing social circumstances and look back to a perceived golden era in the past when things were more perfect. This has been part of the natural rhythm of social affairs as society develops and people find new ways of relating to each other. All change is unsettling for some and there is comfort in supposed past securities and familiarities.

However, it is time to accept the fact that this generation faces something which has accumulated in recent decades and which now adds up to a major social problem. It seems that, as with the shortsighted farmer and industrialist, we have unintentionally taken too much out of the social environment. We have created a hole in the social ozone layer. But, as was the case with the hole in the atmospheric ozone layer, we are slow on the uptake and reluctant to recognize and accept the fact, let alone to do anything about it. A few telling examples are called for. They come not from Balsall Heath, but other parts of the nation.

- **Damilola Taylor.** The heart rending image of this smiley young boy being stabbed by others, then crawling to a lonely, graffiti covered, stairwell to die alone in a Peckham Tower block shocked the nation. His father's agonized scream on the balcony when he saw where his son had died gave more than a pause for thought. It scared the soul.

  Worse, it became clear that many people knew who had done the deed. But nobody with any credibility came forward to speak of it.

- The death of 2 year old **James Bulger** at the hands of two ten year old boys also gripped the nation. Perhaps the most disturbing image of this event was the video footage from the CCTV cameras in the shopping complex where he was abducted. Many adults were present. Some even half held out their hand as if to intervene. But, nobody did so for fear of being thought to interfere. Not long afterwards, his battered body was placed on a railway line and cut in two by a train.

- **Stephen Lawrence** was killed by a group of youths, none of whom have yet been brought to justice and who appear to mock it.

- **Holly and Jessica,** two ten-year-old girls, disappeared one day in Soham. When their bodies were discovered two weeks later they had become so decomposed that their parents could not be asked to identify them in the usual way. The nation had held its breath while hope of their survival still lingered, and then held its head in puzzled sadness when the fatal news unfolded. How could anyone do this? What motive might they have had? What constraints in the social fabric, which might have restrained them, had be come so loose that this act could happen?

Every regional paper carries images from time to time of an elderly man or woman who has been severely beaten either in the street or in their home, robbed of relatively small amounts of money and traumatised for the rest of their lives.

Yet, for every event we know about, there are a thousand others which neither hit the headlines nor even the back page. For, they have become routine.

These are horrific events. They tell the story of everyday life in the nation's excluded 3,000 neighbourhoods, which the Social Exclusion unit identified. Each of them are in their own way like the Balsall Heath of the 1970's which were described in the introduction. But, alone, these stories do not prove that the cathedral crumbles, there is a hole in the social ozone layer or that the nutrients of the social soil have been leached out for short-term gain at the expense of long-term social balance. However, the following statistics do prove it.

Stark statistics

Professor Caridwen Roberts of Oxford University has compiled a number of stark and depressing statistics which show that the family, the corner stone of civil society, is shrinking and, thus, inevitably provides children with less stability and continuity than the development of good character requires. She tells us that:

The population is ageing
- The number of people aged 65 or more increased by 51% in the 40 years between 1961 and 2001.
- The number of children was 23% of the population in 1961. It was 20% in 2001 and is projected to fall to 18% by 2011.

The size of the average household is falling
- The average size was 3 in 1971. By 2002 it had become 2.4.
- While 14% of households had more than 5 people in 1971, only 7% had more than 5 in 2002.
- In 1971, only 18% of households had only 1 person. But, by 2001, this had risen to 29%.

The bonds between a father and mother are fraying
- The average age of first marriage was 25.6 (men) and 23.1 (women) in 1961. It was 30.5 and 28.2 in 2001.

- One in three people aged 36-59 cohabited prior to their first marriage; two out of three people do so in younger age groups.
- More children, 25%, now see their parents divorce or separate before they are 16.
- 40% of live births are now outside marriage.
- There is an increase in childlessness – 15% of women aged 45 in 2000.
- 59% of mothers worked in 1991, while 65% of mothers were in employment in 2001.
- In 1991 prescriptions for anti-depressant drugs totalled 15 million. In 2001 they totalled 24 million.
- Housing benefit is claimed by 14% of all families. But the figure for lone mothers is 55% compared with just 7% for two parent families.

Crime has increased

- Recorded crime has increased by, on average, 5% every year for each of the last 25 years. In Building a Relational Society (Ed, Nicola Barker) Professor A.H. Hasley wrote that:

   "The police recorded 1.6 millions offences in 1970, 2.5 million in 1980 and 5.6 million in 1992. It may be of some comfort to some to know that 95% of these recorded offences were non-violent crimes against property. But it may be of further alarm to others that crime appears on a greater scale when evidence from the 1992 British Crime Survey (based on enquiries in 10,000 English and Welsh households) indicates a total of 15 million crimes a year, many of which were no doubt trivial, and most never reported to the police. One authoritative estimate is that offending rates of juveniles may have increased during the 1980's by as much as 54%. The known offending rate among young people aged 17 but under 21 has, meanwhile, risen by 13%."

   "The records of the police and courts tell us that crime is commonly committed by young men. Over 80% of known offenders are male, and almost half are aged under 21; 1 in 5 is aged under 17. It is known from a study of people born in 1953 that 1 in 3 men, compared with only 8% of women, had been convicted of crimes on a 'standard list' of offences by the age of 35. Offending is clearly more a male than a female characteristic, and this was born out by a Gallup survey of adults and young people in Liverpool and Guildford. General Accident sponsored Gallup in 1993 to survey public attitudes to young people and criminality. Their findings further confirm that contemporary young people are more frequently involved in crime than were their elders or young people in the past."

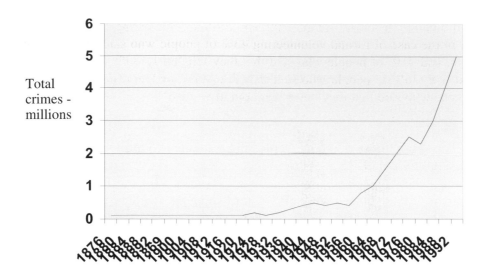

Figure 1: The rising rate of crime

Current age of adults	Estimate of 13-17-year-old crime in their area at the time when they were teenagers (%)
60+	3
35-59	9
25-34	17
18-24	25
	Estimate of 13-17-year-old crime now (%)
Adults	11
Juveniles	43

Figure 2: Estimates of teenagers involved in crime. (Source: Gallup, 1993)

Participation in Voluntary activity

The sense of safety affects whether a person participates in voluntary activities. The Home Offices survey of citizenship (Sept 2003) reports that:

"Unsurprisingly people who said that they felt 'very' or 'fairly' safe in their neighbourhoods were more likely than those who said that they felt 'a bit' or 'very' unsafe and those who said that they never went out after dark to be involved in social participation, informal volunteering and formal volunteering (Figure 3). For example, in the case of formal volunteering 43% of people who said that they felt 'very' safe, and 41% of people who said that they felt 'fairly' safe were involved, compared with 36% of people who said they felt 'a bit' or 'very' unsafe and only 24% of those who said that they never went out after dark."

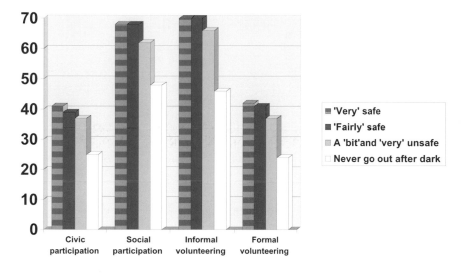

Figure 3: Participation in voluntary and community activities at least once in the last twelve months, by feelings of safety in the neighbourhood.

Are people willing to intervene for the common good?

It is important to consider people's willingness to intervene for the common good. What did they say they did the last time they saw someone drop litter in the street? Fifteen per cent of people said they had intervened and asked the person to pick up the litter and 25% said that they had picked the litter up themselves.

Women were more likely than men to say that they had picked the litter up themselves (28% compared with 22%), and men were more likely than women to say that they had ignored the litter (44% compared with 35%). Older people were more likely than younger people to say that they had picked up the litter. 27% of those aged between 50 and 64 said that they had done so, while only 13% of those aged between 16 and 24 said this.

People who had lived in their neighbourhoods for less than one year were more likely than those who had lived there longer to say that they had ignored the litter (49% compared with 39%, respectively). People who had the lowest household income were more likely than those with the highest income to say this: 49% of those with household incomes less than £5,000 said this, while only 35% of those with household incomes of £75,000 or more did so. People who lived in the most deprived areas were more likely than those who lived in the least deprived areas to say this (48% compared with 32%).

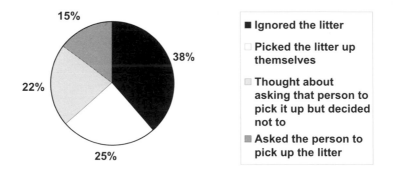

Figure 4: What people did the last time they saw someone drop litter in the street.

Trust in public servants

It is a relief to note that most people still feel able to trust the police and the courts, although a worrying 20% (1 in 5) do not.

However, 50% (1 in 2) do not trust their local Council. Worse, even fewer trust Parliament (33% or only 1 out of every 3 people). Worse still, politicians, those elected to represent people and to run their Council and Parliament are only trusted by 22%, slightly more than just 1 out of every 5 people.

That is, at the same time that Civil Society weakens, there is a very wide and widening gap between people in Civil Society and their political representatives in the public sector or Civic Society. This surely explains why fewer than 60% of people vote in General Elections and less than 30% do so in Council Elections.

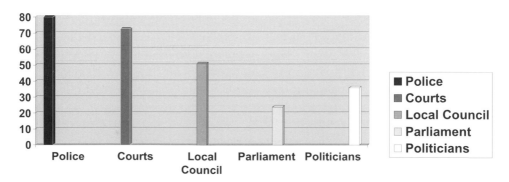

Figure 5: People trusting local and national level public institutions a lot or a fair amount.

So, today:

- More elderly people are cared for in institutions and not within their family.
- More people die alone in hospital.
- Divorce is rising.
- More children are born to single parent families.
- Fewer people know who their neighbour is.
- Fewer people participate in voluntary organisations.
- Despite the vast increase in the police over the last 150 years since the days of the first Constables, crime has also increased substantially.
- Most public open spaces and parks are not well tended and are regarded by the public with trepidation.
- Fewer people vote in both national and local elections.

These problems do not appear so stark in our more affluent areas. Material well-being masks them. So far, they have only become visible and troublesome in materially poor areas where they mingle with other statistics which reveal:

- Poor health
- Poor housing
- High crime
- Poor education
- Poor environment
- High unemployment

Together, they join together to spell out a bleak and despairing prospect for this and the next generation for whom the quality of life leaves a great deal to be desired. For them, the cathedral really does crumble and the gossamer strand has snapped.

All the signs are that while science prolongs life and we now live longer and materially wealthier lives, we also live socially poorer ones in which we care for each other less well and are less fulfilled.

There is a poverty of the human spirit as well as of the general social environment. Worse still, most people do not feel able to do anything to alter their situation. They feel unable to control or improve their life chances and the quality of their social situation.

There is one further factor which causes the greatest concern. Most commentators largely ignore it. The cases of Damilola Taylor, James Bulger and Stephen Lawrence come and go and the above statistics are published. But too few cry halt and ask: What is amiss?

Those who do so are accused by many amongst the chattering classes and the media of 'moral panic' But, they do not live in the neighbourhoods we describe and do not feel the fear or experience the despair. So, they see no more that is of concern with this generation than with any previous one. As with those who dismissed the environmentalists 30 years ago when they warned of the hole in the physical ozone layer, they tell us not to worry and that those who do so are fussing unnecessarily.

Thus, as with the flag which the liberals put down decades ago, the abandoned concern for the quality of life has been picked up by those of an extreme disposition. This has only made it easier for liberal commentators to dismiss the symptoms of social weakness as either a figment of the imagination or a wish to turn the clock back to an illiberal and authoritarian past. They deny that there is a problem.

That is, the problem is ignored and those who identified it are ridiculed, typecast and dismissed. This is a fairly typical avoidance technique. If you don't like the message, shoot the messenger.

Our ability to see through this response is deflected because those same commentators identify the problems which society faces as being the poor material conditions which residents in our inner and outer city areas have to contend with. Indeed, for 40 years, Government has accepted that major problems face people in these areas. It has thrown initiative after initiative and a very large sum of money at the problem but, as we shall see, with little effect. Why?

The answer lies in the fact that the most crushing obstacle standing between these neighbourhoods and renewal is not material poverty, but a social and cultural poverty, a poverty of the soul, the decay of the cathedral. Unless we address this poverty, the hole in the social ozone layer, we will not achieve renewal. So, today's environmentalists of the social scene need to move swiftly from the wings to the centre of the stage and ask:

- Where is our social Rio, our Johannesburg social conference about civil renewal?

- Where are the national and regional debates, which result in the recognition of the need to change the ethos and culture of care and the way we steward the social environment?

- And, where is the best policy and practice to be found, which distils that ethos into a new reality, repairs the hole in the social ozone layer and enables us all to live better, more rewarding and caring lives?

Before we can put matters right, however, we must understand the causes of the problem.

Chapter Three

CAUSES BEFORE CURES

Max Weber, the great German sociologist, taught us that Karl Marx was wrong to suppose that the economy dictated how people thought and what kind of society and culture we lived in. On the contrary, he showed us that ideas have a profound effect on the rest of society, including the economy. Famously, he illustrated how the Protestant Ethic paved the way for Capitalism.

Another related idea has had a profound effect on society in the developed world – that of the Enlightenment. Before the Enlightenment, subjective tradition held sway and the cathedral of society and custom evolved slowly. Elders, grandparents, the priest and scholar, were respected because they knew most about how the universe was ordered, how to behave within it, what was right and wrong. Each new generation looked up to them and, whilst no doubt adapting received wisdom to slowly changing circumstances, the traditions of society evolved and lived on.

The Enlightenment changed all that. In place of subjective tradition, objective reason came to hold sway. The age of scientific enquiry was born in which, quite literally, little or nothing was held to be sacred any more.

It took a few generations for the revolutionary power of objective reason to first take root and then come to hold sway and force subjective tradition and a belief in the moral World of God from the very centre of the stage to the forgotten wings of it. But, although it took a hundred years to supplant subjectivity and enduring value with objectivity and relativity, victory eventually came, and the secular state came with it.

In place of the certainty of the received, inherited, wisdom of tradition, came the uncertainty of relativity in which anything might go and the means justified the end rather than the other way around. Thus, the rational ideas of the Enlightenment created the cultural context in which the once tamed wants of youthful appetites could be set free to deride the traditional judgement of the grandparent, elder or spiritual scholar.

This is not to suggest for a moment that applying objective, scientific, reason to the physical world is inappropriate. Far from it. This has led to profound advances which are mostly for the good. Our understanding of the material world has advanced almost beyond belief. We can now send a rocket to the moon and cure the deadliest of diseases which once cut life short. The problem only arises when we apply the logic of natural science to the subjective social world of tradition and morality. For, they follow a quite different kind of reasoning. Thus, while we can send the rocket to the moon, we can't look after Damilola Taylor or, James Bulger.

Scientific reasoning questions all existing knowledge and constantly tries to find newer, more accurate, ways of analysing reality. New knowledge builds on and replaces old knowledge. So, it is constantly progressing at an ever increasing exponential pace in the way this graph illustrates:

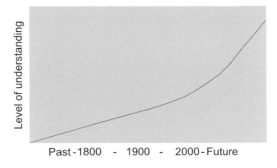

Figure 6: Progress in Science.

We have discovered far more about the material universe in the last 50 years than in all previous human history. Our knowledge is increasing rapidly and it is unthinkable that we might suddenly decide that we might return to a previous mode of thinking, such as when the alchemist tried to turn lead into gold.

Social reasoning follows a quite different kind of logic and, thus, has a different kind of curve of development. Its guiding signposts are not objectively tested laws but subjectively tested ways of behaving to one another whose origins are rooted in the distant past. If we were to draw a graph of social reasoning it would not rise and rise like the one which depicts scientific progress. Rather, it would ebb and flow, rise and fall. It would look like this:

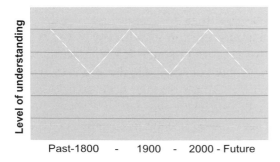

Figure 7: Progress in Social values.

We do not know more now than ever before. Far from it. Degrees of social sophistication come and go. Whilst advances are sometimes made, so also retreats occur. Currently, the suggestion is being made that we are in a period of dangerous retreat. For, we have allowed the logic of science to intrude too far into and unsettle the quite different realm of the social arena. We must re-discover some ancient truths and apply them in modern times.

Technology is the practical application of science. The world has been transformed by it via a myriad marvellous inventions, such as these:

- TV, the fridge and washing machine.
- Computers and instant information.
- Trains, boats, planes and the Internet which have shrunk the world to a global village and enabled us to send rockets to Mars.
- Medicine, drugs, organ transplants and the contraceptive pill.

All these and more have made life many years longer and materially more enriching for most of us. As with the science upon which it is based, technological advance has been good. It has brought very many benefits – you can't get much better than living 30 years longer and having a variety of gadgets to hand which give you an astonishing degree of control over your material environment.

But, again, there are also social downsides. Just as life has been prolonged, we now have powerful weapons of mass destruction which, in the wrong hands, can create untold misery and suffering. Instant information and the global village transform the patchwork quilt of human diversity into the throw away, disposable, world of Macdonalds, trainers and relativity.

As with science, the downside of technological advance can be measured in terms of its adverse affect on the subjective aspect of social and cultural life. We may live materially richer lives. But, it is by no means certain that we live socially better ones. Indeed, as chapter two illustrated, there is compelling evidence that the social bonds which tie us together and make us moral, caring, beings have weakened. The quality of social life has become poorer.

Again, as with science, this is not an argument against technology. It is here to stay and it is important that the quest for ever more sophisticated material tools continues apace. But, there is now a powerful case to be made that the relationship between both science and technology and the social world has become unbalanced to the detriment of the latter and that in future the former must be kept far more firmly in their place. This will entail the substitution of long term social stewarding for instant personal gratification. Success, if it comes, will take real determination and the sustained display of moral courage as we stop taking more out of the social arena than we put back into it.

It is as if there is a social pendulum which, in the past swung too far towards an authoritarian mode of existence and which has been swinging rapidly in recent decades away from this and towards so relaxed a future that children and adults will not receive the care and support they need to live happy and fruitful lives.

For the well-being of children and the future of the social cathedral, we have to find a socially viable medium, a balance between constraint and freedom, which pays due regard to the virtues of both and which is relevant to modern economic and technological conditions. We need to find this balance swiftly before the gossamer strand which Rabbi Neusner spoke of really does snap, it becomes too difficult to reweave it, the hole in the social ozone layer widens and deepens to the detriment of all and the cathedral crumbles and falls.

The point must be emphasised. The Cathedral of civilisation is large and flexible enough to contain within it both science and tradition, objectivity and subjectivity, the world of matter and of the spirit. They are the twin pillars upon which the modern cathedral rests. They are the vital flip sides of the same coin of life. But, if one dominates and the other is subjugated, we all suffer. So, it is very important indeed that we work hard to rebalance the relationship between them so that each can display their respective merits and we ensure that they are even and mutually respecting.

Other Causes of The Problem

There is no one cause of the problems which blight so many of our urban neighbourhoods. Demographic factors are one significant influence. So is the gathering pace of the globalisation of markets. But, one major additional cause has recently been recognised by some which has troubled consciences and accepted political truths. It is the Welfare State itself, the way we manage care for each other and the provision of caring services.

William Beveridge intended social security benefits and pensions to support the workingman and his family only through brief times of sickness and retirement. However, today some people are now unemployed for very long periods and most now live for 20 or 30 years into retirement. The costs of providing so much support for so many people have risen astronomically. Since the Second World War costs have risen from 1% to 13% of GDP, that is, to £95 billion per year. Far more people than ever before are dependant on these state payments. As Frank Field has documented to almost everyone's acceptance, the result is that:

> *"Hard work is penalised by the loss of entitlement. Incentives reinforce welfare dependence. Honesty is punished by a loss of income. It is in this sense that welfare is the enemy within. Its rules actively undermine the moral fabric of our characters. In so doing it eats into the public domain and so helps erode the wider moral order of society."*

Too many people have become dependent on state benefits. They do not see any possibility of getting a job and earning their own money. Their income is derived from taxes paid by others whom they can't see or identify with. Because the state is so large and remote it is seen as impersonal. While a few still will not claim their entitlement out of pride, most do so and many will 'cheat the impersonal system' if they can in a way which they would not do to their personal friends. Now Welfare to Work schemes help, but there is a long way to go before Frank Field's concern is met.

A. Health, Housing, Education, the Environment and Crime

This is not all. There is far more to the Welfare State than benefits and pensions. Since before the beginning of the twentieth Century, caring social reformers also wanted people to have decent housing, a school their children could attend, a National Health Service and a police force – all provided for people by the state and paid for by taxes, hence free at the point of delivery. At the time, this seemed a great advance on the past. The sense of fervour for the collective provision of care for most people built up as the first half of the 20th Century unfolded. It culminated in the reforms made during the Second World War by the coalition Government and by the 1945 Labour Government led by Clement Attlee.

The Conservative Secretary for Education, Rab Butler, put in place the 1944 Education Act. It extended state education for all so that everyone could go to school from 5 to 15 years of age. Aneurin Bevan took just a little longer before devising and putting in place the National Health Service in 1948.

A succession of Labour and Conservative Ministers knocked down the old 'slums' and the huge council estates of the 1950's and 1960's were created. Home Secretary after Home Secretary spent more and more on the police force whose numbers grew apace.

Thus, as I argued in Urban Renaissance, after the Second World War the Welfare State took not so much a step forward as a quantum leap as it advanced on all social fronts. It came to encompass:

*   The provision of Social Benefits including pensions.
*   The provision of houses
*   The provision of education
*   The provision of medical care
*   The provision of safety and order.

In a word, it came to provide care. It took on the maintenance of the social Cathedral.

B. The Private Sector – the Economy

With the benefit of hindsight, the observer might suppose that the material state had expanded far enough by intruding into so many personal, social and educational walks of life. Yet, its ambitions also extended to encompass economic activity. Since the days of Joseph Chamberlain in Birmingham most people had long supposed that 'civic duty' was the best way of building sewers and providing the public utilities of water, gas and electricity. It seemed only a simple logical extension to include the great industries of coal, iron and steel, shipbuilding and the railways. Thus, for almost the whole of the twentieth century, Clause 4 of the Labour Party's constitution committed it to nationalising the 'commanding heights' of the economy as well as providing welfare services covering most aspects of individual, family and communal life.

Indeed, between 1945 and 1978, it seemed that this objective might be realised and that for a civil servant or policy maker to think otherwise was eccentric. Certainly, the post- Attlee Conservative governments of Eden, Macmillan, Home and Heath made no attempt to de-nationalise the large swathes of the economy which had passed into the collective hands of the state and which Harold Macmillan once eloquently and movingly defined as the nation's "family silver".

All governments merely tried to work the same consensual system better than their opponents could. In such circumstances, not surprisingly, the bureaucracies of central and local government grew and grew while the frown on the taxpayer's forehead deepened and despair in those neighbourhoods which concern us took root and multiplied.

C. Funding the Welfare State

Once, taxation was small. It was only used by the state to fund wars and internal security. Today it is large and also funds all the great domestic Departments of State. People are no longer able to decide how to spend a significant portion of what they earn. The caring and 'enlightened' Government of the Welfare State spends it on their behalf in a determined and praiseworthy attempt to make social progress. Social Security benefits now cost the average family £80.00 per week. Add in all other costs and this sum rises to £240.00 per week. This is £12,480 per year. When defence costs are removed, the total spending by the state in Britain on domestic welfare is now £288,000,000,000 and rising.

From this total spending by the State on welfare it is possible to calculate how much of the taxpayer's money is spent on the average excluded neighbourhood of, say 5,000 dwellings, or 15,000 residents. This total is £91, 500,000. The figure is greater, of course, for the typical inner and outer city area. It could be as much as double the average - £183,000,000. Even supposing it is 'only' a little more, say, £100,000,000, this is an astonishing amount of taxpayer's money to spend without actually changing Neighbourhoods of Despair for the better. What is even more surprising is that nobody knows what this figure actually is and that nobody is accountable for it. It is only now that the questions are being posed.

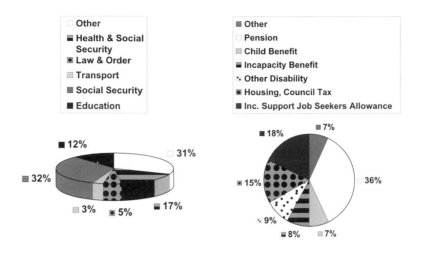

Cost of Benefits	£95,000,000,000
Total cost of all Welfare minus Defence	**£288,000,000,000**

Figure 6: Welfare State – where the money goes.

D. Legitimising the Welfare State
The reasons for the growth, cost and scope of the post-war Welfare State, are various and understandable. They include:

- Compassion. After the ravages of the industrial revolution it seemed sensible and caring to help people who were poor, sick and deprived of many of life's basic amenities by providing things for them.

- Most bureaucracies develop a self-perpetuating momentum. Once created and set in motion they tend to find more and more things to do and to develop an empire. Success is measured in industrial and male terms of size and scope. Understandably, successive governments strove to spend ever more than their predecessors on all aspects of social life.

- As important, perhaps more so, is the way we came to think society worked and how social change or progress could be engineered. For 200 years, a set of assumptions and attitudes, a way of thinking, has been slowly evolving, which tailored the way we set about creating a caring and progressive society. It is worth dwelling on this point for a moment. If we don't, we risk it obstructing our plea to spend the tax payer's money differently.

Copying the rise and rise of the natural sciences, the enlightened founding fathers of sociology supposed that if we looked beneath the variety of 'irrational' traditional social life we could also uncover basic rational social laws which determined people's conduct. It followed, they thought, that if we applied these laws to the government of society then enlightened administrators could produce a similar, ever rising, curve of social progress to match scientific progress. While this view denigrated the concepts of individuality, choice, variety and the notion that people behave in ways which are quite unlike atoms in the physical world, it seemed at first to be both true and to produce social benefits.

Regardless of what people actually thought or believed, the new theory deduced that their action was formed by social circumstances. People did not shape events, they were shaped by them. So, if enlightened politicians and administrators intervened in society and changed the context in which people lived, it would change the people for the better. Thus, for example, if the state increased taxes and redistributed income by boosting benefits and creating institutions – houses, schools, hospitals, police – for all, then it should be possible to make progress and include all in the good life. Politicians were very excited. It seemed that if they redistributed wealth and the state created more and more caring institutions then poverty would be eliminated.

However, a major consequence of 200 years of social 'progress' since the Enlightenment has been that in all vital aspects of ordinary people's lives the balance has slowly shifted from traditional and morally driven 'bottom-up' self-reliant personal/private and neighbourly provision to 'top-down' dependent collective/public provision. What people had once created, sustained and paid for themselves, albeit often glaringly inadequately, gradually came to be provided for them by well meaning politicians of all parties. This provision was no longer delivered as personal, family, or neighbourly gifts or charity, such that the donor expected something in return and the recipient felt obligated to give it, but impersonally through enforced taxation and, thus, via the remote, ever growing bureaucracies of state.

The changing balance from minor state and major private provision of housing, health, education and safety to major state and minor private provisions was not scattered randomly through society. Like other social deprivations, it clustered dramatically in those areas which suffer other ills – the inner and outer areas of our towns and cities and impoverished rural areas. It has become the glue which binds the joined up problems together in these areas and all but creates the self-fulfilling prophecy that people are fashioned by the social situation they are in and can't influence or change it. "If you don't like it, move, there is nothing we can do."

That is, multiple deprivation and joined-up problems feed one further and final concern. It is the most worrying and debilitating of all – the sense of exclusion and the fatalistic powerlessness to do anything to help oneself or to remedy the situation one is in. Most people in the areas we describe feel buffeted by circumstances beyond their control. The only choice open to them is indeed to move, not to change or improve the situation where they live. And few can afford to move. So, those who stay behind can hardly afford to hope. They, like everyone, can dream. But their dreams are dimmed by the despair of everyday reality.

This major characteristic distinguishes troubled modern neighbourhoods from working class industrial pre-war places of material poverty. For, relatively speaking, post-industrial areas are not materially poor. Certainly, this is true if they are compared with their equivalent of the 1920's and 1930's, when the Welfare State was being conceived.

Today, although relatively speaking almost all are materially more affluent, a significant number of people in troubled neighbourhoods lack the capacity, spirit and will to do anything about the problems they face. It is a peculiar irony, therefore, that although such people are materially better off than their counterparts of 100 years ago, they are, in this sense, socially poorer and powerless to help themselves. They suffer a poverty of the soul.

So, it seems that while the enlightenment and scientific objectivity has been with us for 200 years and the last 100 years have been spent in trying to help people out of material poverty we have done the very opposite and created for a significant minority in our society a new kind of social and cultural deprivation – an inability to help themselves and, thus, dependence which is as, if not more, debilitating than economic poverty.

For most of the last century, the shift from personal to impersonal, subjective to rational, moral to value-free, local to national and communal to public was thought to be good and the reason why the curve of social progress would rise sharply in the same way that the curve of scientific progress had done.

As it turns out, people do not fit the theories which ideologies sought to impose upon them. As Osborne and Gaebler have taught us: recent developments show that social laws and collective national plans could work only as long as the politicians and administrators who ran the top-down pyramid like bureaucracies of industrial society "had enough information to take reasonable decisions, which those at the bottom of the pyramid could not query or improve upon; as long as there were mass, undiscriminating markets; as most people had similar needs; as long as the Western industrial nations had no serious competitors which could rival them".

Today, the hierarchical, bureaucratically ordered, world which the social administrator helped to legitimise is fading into the past. As Osbourne and Gaebler point out, in the hi-tech, post-industrial society "people get access to information almost as fast as their leaders do. We now live in a knowledge-based economy in which educated workers bridle at commands and demand high quality and extensive choice." Today it would be no more acceptable for Henry Ford to say to his customers: "You can have a model T car in any colour you want provided it is black" than it is to say: "You can have any pair of spectacles, house or school you want provided it is the off-the-peg pair of National Health specs, estate or school to which your child will be sent."

Osbourne and Gaebler tell us that top-down pyramid-like bureaucracies and institutions which developed during the industrial era increasingly fail us in today's post-industrial society. Today's environment "demands institutions that deliver high-quality goods and services....It demands institutions that are responsive to their customers, offering choices of non-standardised services; that lead by persuasion and incentives rather than commands; that give their employees a sense of meaning and control, even ownership. It demands institutions that empower citizens rather than simply serving them."

Indeed, it demands a very different kind of society from the one which enlightened sociologists felt was inevitable and which, for a while, their theories made universal. And, it requires a different view of how people who live in neighbourhoods of multiple deprivations can realise their hopes and ambitions.

Significant implications
The enlightenment brought reason, objectivity and science into the way we see and can exploit the material world. But it also corroded many traditional, subjective, virtues which restrained and guided our social lives.

Further, while science and technology brought many physical gains it also contributed to the shrinking of the family and deprived an increasing number of young people of the wisdom and experience of elders.

These adverse effects of the otherwise beneficial enlightenment were compounded by the growth of Welfare State which, however, many saw for a long time as being a crowning social achievement, the provision of care for all by the collectively. By degree, however, this took away from many people the sense of responsibility and the virtues of self-help, ownership, dignity and pride.

At first, the benefits of material advance outweighed the harm done to the social bonds which tied people too tightly together in mutual support. But, the effect of the enlightenment is now 200 years old and the Welfare State has been highly developed for sixty years. The long-term effect of both has taken its social toll and become deeply damaging. So, a difficult question arises: How do we retain the benefits of reason and the Welfare State while minimising and overcoming the harm?

Chapter Four

CAPACITY BUILDING
AND SOCIAL CAPITAL

Now that we have considered the problem facing people in excluded neighbourhoods and some of the causes of the problem it is clear that part of the solution is to be found in identifying and empowering Active Citizens. For, without their involvement, renewal will not become sustainable. So, do existing regeneration policies and structures encourage this as not and, if not, what is needed in their place?

A stark, distressing fact stares us in the face. But, we are only just beginning to acknowledge it.

We first noticed that many of our urban areas were in decline 40 years ago. The Urban Aid initiative of the Home Office then became the first of very many successive initiatives aimed at halting and reversing the decline. Since then we have witnessed ICP, SRB 1-7, City Challenge and a host of other initiatives costing many, many, billions of pounds.

However, despite all this, the Social Exclusion Unit (SEU) told us at the beginning of the new Millennium in its report, Bringing Britain Together, that there are now far more excluded neighbourhoods and people than there were 40 years ago and that it is possible to count on the fingers and toes of one person the very few neighbourhoods which have successfully begun the upwards climb to recovery and civil renewal. Three questions arise:

- Just how many billions have been spent, for nobody yet knows?
- Just how can such good intention and hard-earned taxpayer's money have been frittered?
- After so many wasted years what can now be done to put matters right and enable the few recovering neighbourhoods to become many?

Why have Government renewal initiatives not worked?
The reasons why renewal initiatives have not worked so far are becoming clearer. They have tackled the symptom and not the cause. In particular, they have made these cardinal errors:

- **Programmes tended to concentrate on physical renewal and material poverty.** They did not appreciate the social dimension of the poverty of the spirit, the hole in the social ozone layer.

- **Programmes were time-limited to 3-5 years.** Yet, renewal of the spirit and character takes far longer, 20 years longer. A building in the City Centre can be renewed in a year. It takes a generation to rebuild a shattered community. People have not just become materially poor, they have become socially poor. Less visible, more corrosive, this could take a lifetime to alleviate.

- **Funds were 'front loaded'.** In order to gain extra renewal funds from HMG, the professionals who submitted the bid had to say what it was to be spent on and so local people were excluded. By the time they became involved the money had gone.

- **Funds were given to one area after a competitive bidding process, but not to those around it.** Improvements in one area have often been at the expense of surrounding neighbourhoods which have gone into further decline. Those who 'lost' felt excluded and resentment fuelled feelings of jealousy and 'why bother' attitudes.

- **Programmes focused attention on extra or top-up money. They did not address existing mainstream budgets.** We noted that an average neighbourhood of 15,000 people receives £100,000,000 from the state for housing, health, schools, police and benefits every year. These large sums inadvertently create the poor outputs of which people complain. Yet, until very recently, no programme made extra money dependent on disassembling these existing funds and rearranging them in new ways to produce better, more cost-effective outcomes. So, when external funding ended, progress also ended.

- **Renewal programmes were not focused on the neighbourhoods where people live, but on much larger administrative areas defined by planners and politicians.** Renewal is a 'cradle to grave' matter. It turns around the families, neighbours, community networks and places where people live and find their identity and friends. It is about the spirit as well as the body. So, it concerns social areas not the administrative or political ones drawn by those who do not live there. Everywhere the SEU's Policy Action Teams looked, they found that social neighbourhoods have been criss-crossed and confused by planning and administrative boundaries. That is, it turned out that no person or body was responsible for the development of any neighbourhood or accountable for the £100m spent on each of them every year to so little avail. Above all, it was neither managed nor owned by those who lived there.

- **Finally, residents were not in the lead**. The professional and planner in the public sector were seem as the trained, educated, expert. The resident in the community or voluntary sector was the amateur, the beneficiary, not the manager of the process. As people did not feel involved in or own the process of renewal, they did not feel responsible for it or the need to sustain it after it had been and gone.

That is, previous and current attempts at renewal have focused on material deprivation and not on social and cultural deprivation, the need to build people's confidence and the belief that they could act to improve the quality of their own lives.

They focused on worthy top down attempts to help materially poor people but failed to see the need to enable and empower socially poor people to help themselves. This calls for a dramatic change in the way we think about how to care for each other.

- Successful renewal, the SEU concluded, entails putting residents in the lead, building their capacity and confidence and making sure they can talk on equal terms with the planners.

- More than this, capacity building in lonely, fractured, communities in which fear triumphs over hope entails local leaders coming to the fore and creating a new spirit, a new set of relations, which provide the individual with the collective strength needed to change the quality of their lives and then sustain the improvements.

- So, is capacity building and the creation of social capital which will fill the hole in the social ozone layer about volunteering, consultation or something rather more?

Is Capacity Buildings the same as Volunteering?

The body language of volunteering stems from the Culture of Lady Bountiful. She, let us recall, was a lady of leisured means with time on her hands and a good will. She wanted to help people less fortunate than herself. She managed the soup kitchen of the day with dedication and compassion.

Being of means, she did not need to be paid and, quite literally, volunteered to help the needy. Ever since, it has been difficult for the voluntary or third sector to fund its core management/administration costs. Projects could be funded, such as the soup kitchen, but not the supervisor who was supposed to work for love not money.

Don't misunderstand the point; we should have every admiration for the lady. She is as needed today, as yesterday and there is still plenty of scope for such volunteering. But, if we consider her contribution as being sufficient in today's world, we are mistaken. While she has been busy over the last 100 years, two things have happened which have overtaken her and now need to be considered.

First, the Welfare State. It was originally intended to take the place of Lady Bountiful and to look after those who could not help themselves because they had become distressed. But, as the Welfare State grew, it took on more and more of a collective caring role. It came, in effect, to nationalise the way we look after each other in community and civil society. It took away our personal responsibility to be our brother's keeper and did it for us. It gave us rights, but diminished our responsibilities.

The political right understood this partially and came to speak of privatising and individualising care from the nanny state. We, however, understand the need to talk of making the state 'do' less and 'enable' self-help within neighbourhoods. This is not individualism, but mutualism. It entails people taking collective responsibility for each other within the community. If we are to re-discover this language of mutualism we must travel back in time to the roots of socialism in the 1800's when Chartism, the co-operative movement and mutual societies arose.

Second, and complementary to the above, this Third World saying speaks volumes: "How do you help a person who is hungry? Give him a fish and you make him and his family rely on you to give him another fish tomorrow. Thereby, you make him dependent and servile. Yet, teach him how to fish and to make a fishing rod and you make him independent and proud."

No amount of traditional volunteering can help the hungry person to be independent. Nor can the state. The body language of mutual self-help can. It is robust. It creates belonging, ownership and pride. And, it succeeds when we have had precious little success to boast about.

The compelling conclusion to be drawn is that civil renewal, particularly in the neighbourhoods where people live, will not take place either as a result of well meaning volunteers from elsewhere or the state from above, but from the direct involvement of the people who live there. They must manage, own and staff the process of renewal and they must have access to the vast budgets of the disastrous one-size-fits-all services of which everyone complains and which produce dependent servitude.

This is neither volunteering nor privatisation, but the dramatic shifting of power from the state to the local collectivity. It entails building the capacity of the dispossessed to help themselves, to change the circumstances in which they live from ones which blight their lives to ones which transform and liberate them. A new, more balanced, compact between the individual in civil society and the state is implied in which responsibility and the sense of duty is returned to the individual and, perhaps, enshrined in a new concept of what citizenship entails. This is radical. It is exciting, in part, because it works.

So, is Capacity Building the same as Consultation?
There have been honourable exceptions to the failure of previous renewal initiatives. But, generally wave after wave of ABI's (Area Based Initiatives) have involved just a few residents on their Boards, in order to claim in the initial bid for funds that "residents are involved".

Most of these 'resident representatives' have been detached from the rest of the community and, as the programme developed, they have become more and more detached. So, it is not surprising that they were seen by their peers as tokens, were unable to sustain anything when the programme ended and generally gave the term 'community leadership' so bad a name that genuine leaders fight shy of the term. The words and intention of these programmes were well meaning. The practical outcome was negative.

Capacity Building as empowerment and the creation of social capital
Capacity Building has come to describe not volunteering or consultation but empowerment, the process by which residents can combine to make a real difference by playing to each other's strengths, engaging in a range of participatory associations and becoming confident and coherent enough to lead renewal strategies. This entails most or all of the following, although not everyone need engage in more than one or two of them:

- Acquiring knowledge and awareness about what is going on, which can create the sense of inclusion and belonging. For many people, nothing else may be required.

- Seeing the point of becoming a school governor or a Director of a Sure Start project or of a Tenants Coop etc. One resident may become one, another, another.

- Some people are needed to staff or manage the local urban village hall or its nursery or elder's centre. Few deprived neighbourhoods have a vibrant voluntary sector One needs to be created before a neighbourhood can cohere and be regenerated.

- There is the possibility of an incremental capacity, where a mother, for example, starts out by being involved in Sure Start, then becomes a school Governor, then finds the confidence to become the Director of the Local Regeneration Partnership. Again, anyone may stop at any one stage. Few will progress all the way. But, these few must be found and empowered.

- Beyond this, a few people may, as in Tipton, Royds and Balsall Heath aspire to be a Councillor or even an M.P and represent the voice of the community to others.

- Behind and above all these is the role of the facilitator or social entrepreneur, the mini Richard Branson of the social world who "turns other people on" and enables more and more people to become involved in one or more of the ways outlined above, who builds social capital. They might be the chairman of a renewal initiative, or an employee of its Board or have no official title at all.

- Such people used to be the priest or community elder who presided over a communal congregation which celebrated and taught the art and skill entailed in being a responsible citizen. As these people are mostly long gone, the very special role of the community facilitator or entrepreneur or Active Citizen needs to be nourished and developed. It will not, unfortunately, simply grow and multiply on its own. For, without a person or two to play this part, all of the other forms of capacity will be weakened and less likely to develop.

One reason why social capital has leeched from Neighbourhoods is because Christian congregations and priests have become so thin on the ground. However, newcomers from the East have retained the common sense of faith and the social capital of the extended family. They have, therefore, a major positive role to play in helping everyone to become more confident and neighbourhoods to become more robust.

Capacity building takes time – and support

In most excluded neighbourhoods there are many people who know very well what they want – a better life and environment for themselves and their children. But, they are not sure how to achieve this themselves. A teacher, priest or, in their absence, a capacity builder, can show them how. Some practical examples are called for:

- There's a lot of rubbish in the street. A skip costs £70 to hire. No one person would dream of hiring a skip for that amount or of picking up the rubbish themselves. But, if everyone in the street chipped in with £2, joined together in filling it, then hold a street party or barbeque to celebrate, it is possible.

- There is a nuisance neighbour whose children terrify the elderly and keep everyone awake at night. If just one person contacts the police, collects a petition and is prepared to act as a witness, then an Anti-Social Behaviour Order can be served and there is another cause for celebration.

- A stolen car has been abandoned. Its windows are broken and its petrol cap is missing. It is unsightly. All it takes is for one person to know the right council or/and police number and it can be removed.

- Early successes can lead to the formation of a residents group and, perhaps, the acquisition of a community house from a friendly Housing Association or the Council. People can meet and socialise together and plan their next campaign, the opening of a nursery, baby sitting group, Bingo evening, or trip to the seaside.

- Someone might suggest a monthly walk-about the neighbourhood when several residents of the area accompany the police beat officer, housing department manager and environmental service officer. Together, they can spot and deal with a host of minor matters on the spot.

- As others see that small things can be achieved they too will join in, get to know and trust each other. Suddenly a host of things which once seemed impossibly difficult become possible and life can seem positive and hopeful.

In factories, shop stewards help their fellow workers to strive for better working conditions and liase with management to create better working practices and manufacture their product in better ways. It occurred to Trade Unionists who live in Balsall Heath that they could apply their principles of organisation at work in the streets where they live. They call themselves 'Street Stewards.'

- Each street now has a 'Street Steward' and each of 24 sets of streets has a Residents Group with a Chair and Secretary.

- The Street Stewards also help to monitor 15 CCTV cameras from the local police station. They are in discussion with the Police about how they can staff the station's front desk and keep it open 24 hours a day and turn it into a 'Safety Centre'. They run 49 Neighbourhood Watch schemes.

- Each Street Steward knows a variety of useful phone numbers and is able to give informal advice to their neighbours on a range of topics.

- Each steward feeds into and helps to organise their resident's group which is attended by relevant statutory officers who follow up and act on issues raised.

- The 62 streets and 24 residents groups are divided into 4 quarters. Every 2 months a 'walk-about' takes place in each of these quarters. Several street stewards help relevant professional's identify problems such as dumped cars and graffiti and deal with them instantly on the walkabout.

- Some Street Stewards have become so confident and resourceful that they now represent residents via their elected Neighbourhood Forum on various statutory and other bodies.

- On average 23 residents meet in each of the 24 residents groups. So, a total of 552 residents meet every other month.

- Two of the best stewards have gained an HND in management and are on a post graduate course at Birmingham University. They are now employed in regeneration work in support of their voluntary colleagues.

- One of these assists with tailor-made training and support for the Stewards.

- There are dozens of stewards who all receive support. As is clear from the above, some specialise in safety, others in the environment, representation and so on. They all meet together from time to time, often over a meal, to discuss needs and best practice.

- There are now nearly 1,000 members of the Balsall Heath Neighbourhood Forum which acts as the 'Village Voice and Council'. As every resident over 18 years of age is eligible to join the Forum, the present elected executive has set a target of 3,000 members within the year. Already more people vote in Forum elections than in Council ones, although the Forum also aims to double the number of people voting in council elections.

In other places, Street Stewards are called Active Citizens. They are to be found in Salford, Lewisham and elsewhere. But, they do need to be found, supported and encouraged. The kind of infrastructure of voluntary Active Citizens described above can only be created and sustained if at least one Capacity Builder is employed to do so. By this means, precious social capital is built.

Putting a value to Social Capital and the Social Entrepreneur
Empowering active Citizens to build the capacity of many residents of and create social capital is not easy. At least one person needs to be employed full time in each neighbourhood to ensure that it happens and is sustained. How can they be funded?
  These old sayings are pertinent:

'It is a virtue to give but not to count the cost.'
'An economist knows the price of everything and the value of nothing.'

It is easy to cost things in the private sector. Market forces tell us what these costs are. People can then choose whether or not to buy with their hard earned cash the house, car, loaf of bread or whatever is on offer. The job of the private sector entrepreneur is also fairly easy to define and pay for. They have to identify a gap in the market which the customer demands to be filled then design, manufacture and sell the product to the customer. The amount the entrepreneurs can top-slice for themselves and the development of their business will depend on how good and sought after their product is.

However, in the world of social capital 'we live not by saleable bread alone but also by affection and love.' We have never before had to put an economist's price on 'virtue' and 'care'. We simply have not sold them. So, how can we value and pay for the product of the person who manufactures and spreads trust and confidence so that we can employ one in each troubled neighbourhood? For, hitherto, we have 'paid' in similarly non-costed social credits such as praise and respect and used sanctions such as shame.

We may be able to begin to quantify an answer by thinking about the cost of the Welfare State which provides one-size-fits all housing, policing, health, schools and a variety of social benefits to people. Those services which are delivered by public sector professionals using the large budgets of Welfare bureaucracies are being criticised. Public sector housing is ill managed. Crime is too high. Educational performance is poor. Health is poor. The environment is drab. The Government will rise or fall because of what it does about this and whether it succeeds or not in helping to improve the quality of life for most people.

It may be that the quality of these services could be improved simply by managing and delivering them better. But, it is also the case that the caring professions will find this difficult to achieve on their own because the 'customer' is not responsive or confident enough to take full advantage of their efforts. That is, even the best professional is fighting a loosing battle because social capital is so thin that people can't respond effectively.

The professional who delivers these much-criticised services is not happy and does not gain much job satisfaction. The taxpayer certainly isn't happy when he is asked to throw more of his hard earned money at this problem. Thus, they and the Government should be ecstatic if some socially oriented Richard Branson can point the way to success by creating a more responsive social audience and turn the consumer into a producer.

Consider the case of Castle Vale. It was built by the planners of the public sector in the 1950's and 60's. It soon came to vie with Balsall Heath for the title of the least desirable neighbourhood in Birmingham. It was almost entirely made up of municipal housing with over 30 tower blocks.

In 1996 it became a Housing Action Trust (HAT) as residents voted to transfer the housing stock to their own, locally managed, independent Trust. Then, three facts illustrated just how poor conditions were:

- Most residents did not want to live there.
- The unemployment figure was 29%.
- People died seven years sooner than the Birmingham average.

Today, eight years on, these facts have been transformed:

- Most residents now do want to live there.
- The unemployment figure is 5%.
- People now die only two years sooner than the Birmingham average.

These are hugely impressive and important facts which all stem from managing the housing stock differently and enabling local people to gain pride and purpose. The last statistic deserves repetition and emphasis. In the course of eight short years, thousands of people who once died seven years too early, on average now live for five more years. Now that's renewal. That's exciting.

This is of value to the health service, the local health professionals and the Primary Care Trust. It is, of course, quite useful for the individuals themselves. And, it also means that young children benefit from their parent's and grandparent's support for five more crucial years. In one sense, it is not possible to put a price on this achievement. It is simply invaluable. In another, it is very easy to do so. Ask people who live or work in other areas what they would pay for five more years. The answer is probably: "Just tell us what it costs and we'll pay it." And, the answer to that is: "Not a lot". It entails managing the housing stock differently, deploying some health professionals and their resources differently and, literally, giving local people a fresh will to live, the capacity to live healthier lives, the ability to fish and make their fishing rod.

What product can the Capacity Builder manufacture which their public sector partners can value and put a price on?
The employed Capacity Builder can offer a range of interconnected services.

- In place of a passive, unresponsive, community the Capacity Builder can provide all partners with a responsive, receptive, and well-organised community which will make their statutory role more pleasant, focused and productive.

- The Capacity Builder can enable residents to undertake a scrutiny role which can challenge partners to deliver a more appropriate, tailor made, and targeted service to a locally derived agenda.

- The Capacity Builder can also employ local people to deliver some essential para-professional services.

- The Capacity Builder can thus generate the sense of pride and ownership, which creates a 'feel good' factor and sustains the kind of 'confidence' in which any agency can flourish.

- The Capacity Builder can motivate and empower residents to train and become employed by any of the local caring professions.

- The Capacity Builder can help to redraw administratively convenient, but inappropriate, boundaries so that they coincide with the social boundaries within which people live in neighbourhoods.

- The Capacity Builder can then help all partners to join their otherwise distinct, uncoordinated, actions together to develop best practices in neighbourhood management and effective budgeting.

- The Capacity Builder will also work with their private sector counterparts to develop a private-public-community sector partnership which will manage and develop underused, undervalued, local assets productively.

- That is, the Capacity Builder relieves the statutory professional of the need to deliver all services and thus do nothing very well and enables them to concentrate on delivering those services which only they can provide and so do 'less, but better.'

Agreements between the capacity builder and their public and private sector partners

Service level agreements can be made between the capacity builder, their resident employers and their public sector partners, which aim to achieve the following kinds of results:

- **Police**
  Crime will fall by 10% each year. 10% more people will feel safe each year.

- **Housing**
  House prices will rise. There will be less than 2% of voids.

- **Health**
  People will live 2 years longer within 4 years.

- **Parks**
  10% more people per year will say the environment is improving.

- **Education**
  S.A.T's results will improve by 10% per year.

- **Fire service**
  10% more houses per year will have smoke alarms.

- **Businesses**
  Insurance premiums will be reduced in 5 years by 10%.

- **Environment**
  Litter will be reduced and graffiti will become non-existent within 12 months.

Putting a price to the agreements

We have always paid the voluntary sector priest and provided him with a home. But, the faithful paid for him by means of a deliberate and personal donation. And, he was trained and supported by the wider church with its special traditions and hierarchies.

It is, in part, because we can no longer rely on the church and the priest to sustain us in spiritual communion with each other that we need to develop the new more secular role of social entrepreneur or Capacity Builder. Like the priest, he or she, will lead and guide the way we relate to each other, care for the young, respect and look after the elderly. Equally, like the priest, he or she will need to involve us all in a variety of collective and mutually beneficial ways for which we will not be paid. Further, we will be expected to invest time and money in the creation of social capital.

This means the Capacity Builder must accept a very special responsibility and fulfil a very particular duty. Their role is as close that the secular can get to becoming the sacred. The Capacity Builder will, therefore, feel a particular affinity with the priest. Prince Charles wishes to become Defender of Faiths and not of the faith. The Capacity Builder is the defender, advocate and multiplier of faith in the community and hope in the future.

So, as with the priest, it is symbolically very important that they are remunerated by the community in which they work and not by some distant bureaucracy. Just as the communion of the faithful pays the priest, so the Capacity Builder must be paid by the neighbourhood within which they work from a budget which is detached from the Welfare State and given to a new kind of neighbourhood authority. This budget is not derived from an external grant but from statutory players who see the point in investing a fraction of their own mainstream budget in building a strong, resilient neighbourhood. The next chapter details how this can be done.

Capacity Builders and leadership

Good leadership is important in all walks of life. A good head can make all the difference between a good, high achieving, and a failing school. The same is true of the head of the Housing Association, Primary Care Trust, and police divisions, the Church or Mosque.

Yet all these agencies already exist. They have a building, staff, budget and a defined service to deliver. All that the good head of the service has to do is to organise their existing staff, resources and budget well, provide a good service to their customers and report and respond to their accountable body.

This is not always easy. Colleagues often carp and need motivating. Budgets are never sufficient; a little more for one thing always has to be found by making do with less in some other area. Those to whom one reports can help or be unkindly critical and make it that bit more difficult to manage the whole team. But, it is relatively straightforward. The path is already there to follow. It has been travelled many times before and it will be taken many times again.

Further, because the path is there, the job known and the budget in place, when the Head of an existing institution leaves, it is also relatively easy to find a replacement. There is a natural pool from which to recruit. A large school might look for a replacement from the deputy of another large school or the head of a smaller one. Teachers on the look out for a career move know which journals to look read and, once appointed, all the trappings and needs of office are at hand.

Leadership in the field of Civil Renewal carries extra burdens

Leadership in the civil and neighbourhood renewal business requires additional skills. For, except in the recent 40 NDC and 30 Neighbourhood Management Government funded pathfinder areas, there is no budget for renewal, no team, no neighbourhood plan, no accountable body. In each of the other 2,930 non-grants aided, excluded, neighbourhoods these essential requirements all have to be assembled from nothing, magically materialised from nowhere.

On the one hand, unconfident residents have to be persuaded that they can make a difference, can help to shape priorities and services and show statutory professionals how to proceed. On the other, professionals have to be shown how to move from 'doing' to 'enabling' mode, re-work established ways of behaving, allocate budgets, report to their elected representatives and deliver a radically different, far more effective, product.

That is, the Capacity Builder not only has to find their own budget, create a team and other resources from scratch, they also have to create their own job from nothing and find a way of multiplying that job so that other neighbourhoods can also be served. For, nobody has done the job before. Hitherto, the profession of the social entrepreneur has not existed. Creating your own job is difficult. And it is risky. This is almost unheard of in the public sector. It's made even more difficult and risky because, as progress is made in making something from nothing and managing change, those content with the status quo will be disturbed. They will place obstacles in the way. Some instances are in order.

Token residents

The task of including more and more residents in the process of civil renewal and the management of their neighbourhood can be hindered by one or two token residents whose pride has been boosted by professionals who have used them in place of genuine, widespread, participation. They wish to cling to their status but have to be persuaded to stand aside to allow others to come forward. And, if they won't move willingly, they have to be moved unwillingly.

They are, of course, likely to create a fuss about this, cry foul and appeal to those professionals who also don't want change and Councillors who are not yet aware of the etiquette of the new politics of renewal.

Professionals who 'do' but can't 'enable'

Some professionals can be just as obstinate as token residents. They wonder why they should have to re-work their budget, relinquish parts of it to a neighbourhood team, treat residents as equals, work with them to develop and implement a neighbourhood plan when, until now, they were content to deliver a one-size-fits-all service.

A change-delaying nuisance in their own right, such professionals can be even more of a headache to the capacity builder when they team up with those token residents who also feel their interests lie in slowing the pace of change. There can be even greater difficulties, however. For, some Councillors also feel their interest rests in preserving the status quo.

Councillors

Some Councillors can be astonishingly supportive of Civil Renewal. They can make the difference between real progress and stagnation. But, regardless of their party, some can also positively hinder renewal and make life almost impossibly difficult for those who seek progress.

Like the proud token resident and defensive professional, the Councillor can persuade themselves that they and they alone are 'an important person'. Instead of listening to others they feel the need to tell them what to do and how to behave. When others assert themselves and begin to devise an agenda for local action, they stand in its way and insist that they, as the locally elected representative, know best.

Of course, it is precisely this sad attitude which has got local politics a bad name. It explains why less than 20% of residents vote in local elections in some excluded areas and why so many feel that the credibility gap between the people and their political representatives is unbridgeable.

The forces of the token residents, defensive professional and the conventionally minded councillor have often combined to slow and defeat most renewal initiatives in the past. Both separately and together, they have out manoeuvred many a budding capacity builder. But, there is one more player on the field of civil renewal whose action makes it even easier to slow the process of change – the criminal.

Criminals

Some sophisticated innocents who do not live in the nation's 3,000 excluded neighbourhoods do not realise the extent to which a few criminals can hold an entire neighbourhood in a kind of frightened captivity.

As in the case of James Bulger, Damilola Taylor or Stephen Lawrence, just one person or one family let alone a couple of dozen people can hold 10,000 people in a neighbourhood in fear and trembling so they can pursue unhindered their life of crime and anti-social behaviour. As they say, all it takes for evil to triumph is for good people to do nothing. And, if the good people have tried but the police, housing and other authorities have not acted with sufficient determination, then it can make sense for ordinary residents to give up, submit or move out. Either way, this merely feeds the appetite of the criminal and encourages them to be even more aggressive and threatening.

The result is that residents who feel frightened won't attend meetings, can't believe the quality of their lives can be improved and will refuse the entreaties of the capacity builder to become involved. Thus, in joining an unholy (but coincidental) alliance, the criminal can help token residents, professionals and Councillors to prevent residents from gaining the confidence and acting to build a strong community.

That is, things will stay the same – unless the capacity builder can outwit this alliance whilst also creating their own job! No easy task – without real support.

Turning defeat into victory

There are additional reasons why so few neighbourhoods have been renewed. But, the players described above are surely sufficient to convince most people that the capacity builder needs to possess remarkable qualities of patience and leadership if they are to succeed in kindling the civil renewal of a neighbourhood.

It is little wonder that, so far, very few have succeeded. Given the odds against success, many have either not even tried or been set back by one or other or all of the above.

We are, in effect, considering the most effective ways of changing the way we have delivered care to each other for 60 plus years. That is, we are talking about 'regime change.' This will not happen just because government or we identify the need for it or ask for it to take place voluntarily. It must be made to happen with determination.

Success requires that we rely not just on 20 remarkable leaders, but that we find and support 3,000 plus ones who are all able to turn civil renewal from being the exception to becoming as routine as, say, teaching in schools. If we are to persuade good people to play this leadership role we must make it easier for them by levelling the playing field in two ways:

First, the Government really must help by changing the structure and culture through which renewal is delivered. In place of individual capacity builders having to muster their own budget and teams, these must be made available as a matter of necessity.

Second, the first wave of Capacity Builders must be helped to set up a series of networks which support a second and third wave of practitioners and make it easier for them to avoid the pitfalls described above so that they can make rapid progress.

Government intervention
Very clear guidance is needed from Central Government to LSP's and from LSP's to statutory players about the need to support Capacity Builders.

Equally clear guidance is needed for Councillors about their role. Perhaps it is time to issue them with a Job Description and clear advice about how to help not hinder residents in their Ward.

Support networks and training
Many Capacity Builders are very isolated. They have personally experienced one or more of the difficulties described above. They have been puzzled and bruised by them and have not witnessed on the ground the results which policy makers in Whitehall intended. Making progress against such odds can seem so difficult and lonely a task that many wonder whether its worth the strain and effort.

That's why so many who struggle in excluded neighbourhoods have visited the few success stories which exist and asked: "How did you do that?" Through such visits less experienced, hesitant, residents and others have discover that persistence can result in progress. If this or that professional, obdurate token resident, truculent Councillor and criminal gang can be defeated in Royds or Toxteth, Peckham or Castle Vale the visitors can come to believe that they too can succeed.

We are probably in the early stages of the formation of a new association of civil renewal workers, a new profession of Capacity Builders. Circumstances must have been similar when the first work place unions were being formed and the first shop steward in one factory visited or were visited by workers in an un-unionised factory who asked: "What did you do to gain better conditions? How did you persuade the manager/ owner to listen to your requests?" Today, of course, stewards in the local factory are supported by regional and national coordinators. Regular training courses are available. Capacity Builders require no less.

In anticipation of the need for mutually supportive associations, the ODPM has set up a series of Regional Centres of Excellence and the Home Office has founded a Centre for Active Citizenship. These are, in effect a virtual, dispersed, school or association of renewal which recruits, trains and allocates experienced practitioners to new neighbourhoods in need of renewal. Before he died, the astonishingly inventive David Young, created a School for Social Entrepreneurs in London's East End. As discussed in chapter six, a variety of other training centres and networks exist – Trafford Hall, The Regen School, Community Matters and, of course, experienced residents from the few recovering neighbourhoods.

So, we don't need a new association or training centre when so many pieces of a jigsaw of support are already in place. But, we probably do need to give added point and purpose to what exists if the picture is to be completed. So, it may be sensible to challenge existing players to discuss with each other ways of providing a series of meeting places and courses which are tailor-made to support the growing task force of active citizens and enabling professionals.

Joining the bottom-up capacity builder to the top-down neighbourhood manager
The greatest help for the capacity builder will come through managing statutory services differently. The really exciting prospect is to link the bottom-up creativity of the Capacity Builder with the top-down ingenuity of a Civic Entrepreneur. Castle Vale has achieved wonders through managing its housing stock differently. Can we achieve similar things in other neighbourhoods by not just managing housing but also other services differently? If we can, we will probably have solved the puzzle of how to make life easier and more straight forward for the hard pressed capacity builder. If this chapter has been about managing and organising residents in the voluntary sector differently, managing the public sector services and budgets of neighbourhoods differently is the subject of the next chapter.

Chapter Five

FUNDING AND MANAGING CIVIL RENEWAL

The Bottom-up renewal of civil society by Active Citizens helped by Capacity Builders is only on one half of the process of neighbourhood renewal. In some neighbourhoods Active Citizens can and have built wonderful new association which have made the quality of life far more attractive for their families and neighbours. But, it will be difficult, if not impossible, to sustain that quality and for Active Citizens to replicate it in many neighbourhoods unless it is also possible to get the Top-Down delivery of services by Civic Society to work in supportive, mutually productive, alignment with them.

This will not be easy. For, Civic Society, the Welfare State, has not previously recognised the need to relate to neighbourhoods nor to empower and work in partnership with residents. It has been organised quite differently to suit other requirements. However, a start has been made. The first foundations have been laid and can be built upon.

In the past, we have thought that a major reason why 3,000 neighbourhoods had become excluded was because not enough tax payer's money had been spent on them. So, a series of costly Central Government renewal initiatives were needed to provide this extra money. Thus, two questions become relevant:

- How much Urban Aid has been spent over the last 40 years?
- Has it worked? How many neighbourhoods have been renewed by it?

The answer to question one is not yet known. But, the Home Office started to spend many tens of millions each year 40 years, ago. Inner City Partnership increased the amount of this aid via the Department of Environment. Then came 7 rounds of SRB. Currently ODPM funds 39 New Deal Community areas. Each are in receipt of £50m over 10 years, which is £1,950,000,000. A further, 88 Local Authority areas receive the £800,000,000 of Neighbourhood Renewal Fund. This has been extended for another two years. In addition, the Government's Health, Home Office, Education and other departments all have their own spending initiatives. So, the global answer has to be that many billions upon billions of extra pounds have been allocated to blighted areas on top of existing mainstream budgets.

In the light of such vast sums, the answer to the second question, how many neighbourhoods has this vast sum successfully renewed, thus seems even more important. After all this extra money has been spent, it is depressing to record that the Social Exclusion Unit reported that there are now more excluded neighbourhoods than ever before. Yet, there are just 20-30 neighbourhoods in the country which are en route to successful renewal and most of them report that this success was achieved despite and not because of the 'system'. It seems that the massive top-up renewal grants have had little or no effect and that, hitherto, the Active Citizen and Capacity Builder has had little or so support.

Perhaps, then, it is relevant to put aside the top-up renewal initiatives for a moment and remind ourselves about just how much money is routinely going into each failing neighbourhood each year via the existing mainstream budgets and services of the statutory agencies of the Welfare State. For, if extra money has little effect, perhaps the explanation of the problem lies not in the need for new money, but in the way existing money is spent.

When the author first asked the question to Birmingham Council officials nobody knew the answer. "But", they said: "We can tell you what the whole of Birmingham Council and different departments spend. So, Central Government officials were asked, then ministers. It turned out that nobody knew the answer, although one minister said: "But, it's an interesting question. If you find the answer, let me know."

Before reminding ourselves as to the answer, it's important to consider why the question hadn't been asked before. It is simple. Neither Central nor Local Government, nor the police authority nor health trusts spend money in relation to the neighbourhoods where real people live. Rather, they spend and deliver services in terms of the political wards and other bureaucratically convenient boundaries through which they administer these services. – See figure 10.

While a typical neighbourhood might be made up of just15,000 people, a typical administrative area might contain anywhere between 50,000 and 100,000 people, sometime rather more. Of course, the budgets which are spent in these large administrative areas are all accounted for impeccably and to the last penny. However, when we come to consider the outcome of this spending in neighbourhoods, these vast sums actually contribute to the high crime, high unemployment and blight from which real people suffer.

It is now clearer why the billions and billions of extra top-up renewal funding for initiatives simply vanished, as if down a drain, to little effect. It is not the case that there wasn't enough existing money to produce good services and renew neighbourhoods and that more would make a real difference. Rather, the existing money was not well targeted on real people in real neighbourhoods and extra renewal money simply disappeared with it. So, the solution to renewal lies not in extra money, but in using existing money very differently.

That's why it's so important to know what is spent in each neighbourhood. Can it be disentangled from the different administrative zones via which the Welfare State's statutory services and benefits are allocated and reassembled in the neighbourhoods where people live?

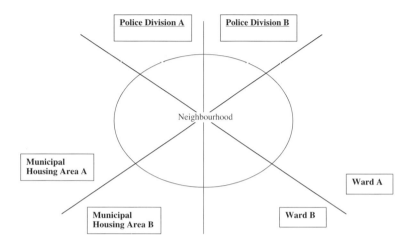

Figure 9: Any one social neighbourhood is criss-crossed and divided by many lines of governance.

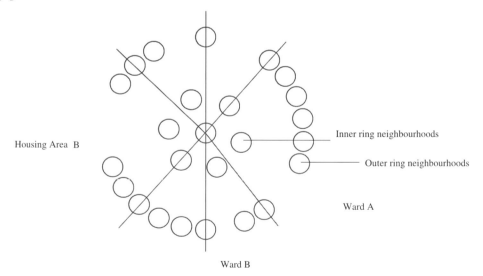

Figure 10: Any one urban authority area is made up of many neighbourhoods. It looks something like this. But, none of the neighbourhood boundaries fit with those defined by the bureaucracies of the service deliverers.

The neighbourhood budget – and the neighbourhood bursar or treasurer

The Government of the day asked the Civil Service in the early 1980's what a school cost. It wondered if each school's budget could be passed to it and whether schools could be locally managed (LM). At first, the officials did not understand the question. They answered in terms of just hundreds of pounds and referred to dinner money and jumble sales. The Government persisted. It asked what the school's buildings and teachers cost, the full budget. At the time, of course, this was invisibly consumed within the Local Education Authority's (LEA) budget. It managed all schools, none of which had their own budget or even knew what it was.

Finally, the question was answered properly. We now know that a typical primary can cost £800,000 and a secondary £2,500,000 or more. Further, each school now has 90% of this budget. In place of a remote LEA taking Top Down one-size-fits-all decisions on behalf of all schools, each school takes it own particular decision about just how much to spend on chalk, computers, books, teachers etc – and they are much better for it. Further, in place of just 15 Councillors elected via Wards controlling the way civil servants managed schools, now 15 ordinary people sit on the Governing Body of each school. In a Local Authority area of, say, 200 schools, that is 3,000 people who are involved in place of just 15. That's subsidiarity! It's also empowerment.

When the question about 'what does a neighbourhood cost' was first posed, officials responded in a similar way to the way education officials first answered the same question about schools. Nobody knew, because the different bits and pieces of what a neighbourhood cost were absorbed within the far wider budgets of the statutory silos of police, health and local authority departments.

However, when each neighbourhood's fraction of these huge, far wider, statutory budgets is detached, we now know that it adds up to a staggering £100,000,000 plus, per year per neighbourhood of 15,000 people.

Yet, to date, this sum has been invisible. It does not exist in practice and, therefore, nobody has been accountable for it. It is very important to make it visible, to disentangle it from the wider budgets of each statutory agency. Of course, some of it will always have to relate back to the far wider administrative area from which we have just theoretically detached it. Some bits and pieces can't be delegated to the neighbourhood's level of subsidiarity. For example, there can only be one Chief Constable, one University, one General Hospital etc, etc. So, some of the neighbourhood's sum has to be retained centrally to pay for them. When this top slicing has taken place, what fraction of the £100,000,000 can be devolved to each neighbourhood? Is it the 90% which schools now get, leaving the Chief Education's Officer with just 10%. Or, does rather more have to be retained?

Let's suppose that 50% has to be retained, at least to start with. That leaves £50,000,000 which can be got right down to neighbourhood level. Now, of course, some of that is still fairly inflexible and spoken for. For example, each school will still wish to retain its budget and the cutting of the park's grass will still require the driving of the mowing machine.

So, for the sake of the argument, let's also suppose that most of the £50,000,000 will at first be relatively fixed, say, 98% of it. This leaves us with two important considerations:

1. First, the 98% or £49,000,000 which is 'relatively fixed' can be used in imaginative, slightly different, ways. For example. Instead of say, the 5 primary schools on the patch (total cost 5 x £800,000 = £4,000,000) all advertising separately for a new teacher, they might advertise jointly. They might pursue a common procurement policy and get the park mower to also mow their grass etc.

   Other schools in other neighbourhoods may respond quite differently. One set might even create a Family Centre which is able to teach parenting skills. The scope and implications are enormous and diverse.

2. Second, the remaining 2%, just 1% of the total budget which can initially be used differently amounts to £1,000,000 for each and every year. Although it is at this stage a tiny percentage, it is an enormous sum which the neighbourhood could not previously access. Yet, it is potentially available for the pursuit of the civil renewal agenda for each and every year and for each and every neighbourhood in the land. That bears repetition and emphasis, as follows:

This sum of £1,000,000 can be found within existing mainstream budgets. It dwarfs even the largest external top up sums spent on renewal over the last 40 years. But, in place of 'more of the same' failing way of spending it, we are forced to spend it in ways which link with the places where people live. It engages their attention. It is owned and accountable. Consider the future. When new managers of these sums have been at work for a few years, they will find even more exciting ways of using the 'spoken for' £49,000,000 and ways of detaching more than 2% of it. Ten percent would give them £5,000,000 a year to further rebuild the social fabric of the neighbourhood. That is, if we begin to manage neighbourhoods in this way, we could give every neighbourhood in the country the kinds of sums we currently give to just 39 NDC areas without troubling the taxpayer.

Further, we can account for that budget and spend it with the help and advice of a Neighbourhood Bursar or Treasurer.

A Neighbourhood Development Plan

We are familiar with the idea of a business having a business development plan. Schools now have school improvement or school development plans. So do most agencies worth their salt. Yet, up to now, it is possible to count on the fingers of one hand the neighbourhoods in the country which have a Neighbourhood Development Plan.

This can't make sense. Just what would we say about a business which cost £100,000,000 per year which did not have a development plan? Within seconds it would be closed down and reopened under new, more competent, management. In effect, that's what we are saying about neighbourhoods. They have been managed so ineffectively that they have, quite literally, not been managed at all. Thus, a new way of managing them should be devised and put in place as swiftly as possible.

It is common sense really. Each neighbourhood needs to work out a Neighbourhood Development Plan or its residents and the agencies which service them will not know what targets they are aiming to achieve, whether they are falling short or improving, what they are costing or if they are worth it. Each Neighbourhood Development Plan will need to be ambitious if it aims to turn the whole area round within, say, five years and then sustain progress. It will need to address all of the subjects and set ambitious targets, such those which are outlined in figure 11 below/over page.

Area	Key Players	Target	Review date
The family	All relevant agencies and key residents representatives	Help, say, 100 families. Create parent centres in every primary school	In 12 months time
Health	All relevant agencies and key resident representatives	Reduce infant mortality by 20%. Set up, healthy living centres	In 12 months time
The House	All relevant agencies and key resident representatives	Involve all tenants in management of the house	In 12 months time
The school	All relevant agencies and key resident representatives	Improve standards by 30%. Cluster and pool resources	In 12 months time

contin...

Area	Key Players	Target	Review date
Employment	All relevant agencies and key residents representatives	Reduce unemployment by 50%	In 12 months time
Crime	All relevant agencies and key residents representatives	Reduce crime by 50%	In 12 months time
The environment	All relevant agencies and key residents representatives	Clear the litter remove the graffiti	In 12 months time
Mutual associations	All relevant agencies and key residents representatives	Enable all the residents to help each other at a very local level	In 12 months time
Assets	All relevant agencies and key residents representatives	Take ownership of key parks, lands and buildings	In 12 months time
Neighbourhoods management	All relevant agencies and key residents representatives	All key agencies to be actively involved	In 12 months time
Partnership between residents and statutory agencies	All relevant agencies and key residents representatives	The bottom-up and top-down to be playing fully to each others strengths	In 12 months time
Quality review and inspection	All relevant agencies and key residents representatives	Set new plan and new targets in 1 year's time. Identify strengths and weakness	In 12 months time

Figure 11: Chart of Neighbourhood Development Plan.

If the targets which each neighbourhood's plan outlines are achieved, then it should be possible to turn a failing area round in a few years in just the same way we now know a failing school can be turned into a successful one. All that is required is:

- A budget
- Good management by one Capacity Builder and one Neighbourhood Manager with the help of a Bursar - and support staff
- Clear sighted aims and targets – a plan
- Enthusiasm and will for everyone involved
- Inspection, sanction and praise by the local authority and residents forum
- Partnerships based on trust and understanding

Perhaps later years and later stages of the Neighbourhood Development Plan will include the ownership and management of real assets by local people. These will include land, buildings and, above all, the employment of local people. When, and if, this advanced stage is reached, some community associations, enterprises or trusts may well themselves take on the delivery of such key services as:

- Care in the community
- Some Social Services such as elderly day care
- Some Leisure Services
- Schools
- Houses
- Environmental works
- Community enterprises and job creation
- Aspects of community safety

Schools are now controlled by Governors drawn from the local area and many housing estates are managed by tenants. The question to ask, therefore, is not which services might be passed to local people to manage, but which should not be delivered in this way.

The neighbourhood needs a manger

You might think it is surprising that up to now we did not know what the budget of cach neighbourhood was. But, it is even more of a shock to realise that we did not have a development plan, which explained how that money would be spent. Further, until very recently no neighbourhood had a neighbourhood manager who was responsible for the quality of services delivered or accountable for the large sums of public money they cost – or for the maintenance and strategic use of public assets, buildings and land.

It is important to press the point. To continue our analogy with schools, if they were run in the way neighbourhoods are run, they would have:

• No visible budget.
• Nobody to account for the budget.
• No development plan for spending that budget or improving standards.
• No head-teacher.

Just how did we devise such a peculiar way of looking after such large sums of money and why have we not questioned it for so long? Better late than never. We can now see that in addition to a Capacity Builder, Neighbourhood Forum and Development Plan each troubled neighbourhood also needs a senior Neighbourhood Manager who will be responsible for ensuring that top-down services are joined up and directed at the targets set by Development Plan.

A Neighbourhood Manager might be appointed or seconded from the ranks of local authority officers or, they might come from outside the local authority. Indeed, it is important that many come from industry, the police or health professionals to whom they will have to relate just as directly as any local authority department.

It is important to remember that 3,000 plus of these senior managers will eventually be needed, one for each excluded neighbourhood. It will not be easy to identify, recruit, train and support so many, especially as they will have to be independent spirits able to rise to daunting challenges and to manage themselves as well as their inter-agency neighbourhood team. Someone who was previously trapped and frustrated within the Local Authority may surprise us all. Equally, someone who was experienced in setting- up and running the new branch of an expanding business may have a head start.

Crucially, the senior Manager will need to think in new ways, bang established heads together, assemble an inter- agency team of players able to help the Capacity Builder and Forum to deliver the Neighbourhood Development Plan, meet and improve upon ambitious targets.

Education Action Zones have an educational supremo who is valued at £60/70k. The head of a secondary school with a budget of £2.5m can earn £60k - £80k. The Manager of a neighbourhood on which £100m is spent should be paid £80k or more. The right calibre of person must be attracted and all concerned will know that they have the stature, status and determination to succeed where all others have not even tried.

The senior neighbourhood manager of statutory services will wish to:

• Work closely with his/her Capacity Builder counterpart. Together, they are the flip sides of the coin of Neighbourhood Management.

- Assist The Forum with the annual preparation and review of the neighbourhood development plan.
- Ensure that the statutory components and targets of that plan are hit and improved upon.
- Enable the Community's Capacity Builder and local associations to trade with devolved statutory services and, where appropriate, undertake some of these services.
- Help the Local Authority to move from a situation where the community sector is dependent on time-limited grants and regeneration initiatives to one where they can trade with the public and private sectors, build sustainable community enterprises, jobs and a vibrant hinterland.
- Report to a delivery board which is community-led by the Neighbourhood Forum.

The Senior Manager will need to choose an inter-agency Neighbourhood Team of officers from amongst the existing staff of different Local Authority departments as well as from other strategic partners such as the Police, RSL's and the PCT and ensure that they play to each other's strengths as well as those of the community.

At first, this team or Neighbourhood Strategic Partnership may well help existing specialist service providers to improve the quality of that provision. By degrees, however, a number of these services may be passed to the community to deliver.

The 'top down' and the 'bottom up' are interdependent
Some professionals and policy makers have suggested that it is sufficient to reorganise the top-down into the neighbourhood management teams described above. These, it is said, will deliver the goods and that a new form of bottom- up response from the community is unnecessary and too prescriptive. Why should communities be expected and encourage to behave with such a degree of responsibility?

This question is ill-considered. It does not make practical sense. Even the most sensitive and caring service which is delivered 'for' people still makes them dependent and unable to help themselves. It de-skills and de-motives them. It conveys the message: 'you have rights, but no responsibilities, you can't fish.'

Thus, it makes the task of even the well motivated professional difficult if not impossible and further atrophies the spirit and quality of life in neighbourhoods.

If inner and outer city areas are to recover and if people are to be empowered to take control of and shape their lives, then sophisticated new forms of local mutual associations and participatory representation are quite essential ingredients of a new top-down, bottom-up partnership. That is, the flip side of the coin of the civic entrepreneur and neighbourhood management is the Capacity

Builder who forges and fastens the communal bonds within the neighbourhood and makes it responsive to well delivered neighbourhood services to the point where some of these are delivered or managed by local people.

It is possible to picture the relationships between the bottom – up and top – down, the Capacity Builder or Civil Entrepreneur and the Neighbourhood Manager or Civic Entrepreneur as follows:

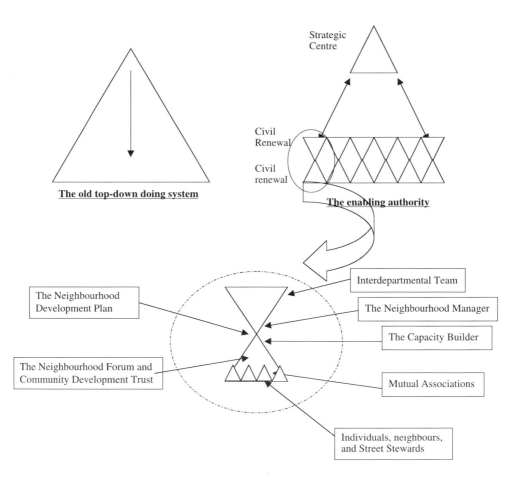

Figure 12: The Structure of Neighbourhood Management

The costs of Capacity Building and Neighbourhood Management

Each neighbourhood will deploy its £31m differently. But, the initial Cost of the Community's Capacity Builder and the Senior Neighbourhood Manager can be suggested as follows:

The initial needs of the Capacity Builder

Bottom-up Forum

The Capacity Builder (Social Entrepreneur)	50
Sec/Admin	25
Safety officer	19
Environment officer	19
Special projects	70
Running Costs for Street Stewards	20

Total   £203k

The costs of the Neighbourhood's Management Team

Top-Down Neighbourhood Management

Senior Manager (Civic Entrepreneur)	80
Secretary	15
Team identified from within all relevant departments & seconded	-
Running Costs	35

Total   £130k

Grand Total   £333k

In addition to these initial costs those of new developments which the Capacity Builder will create should be considered. These might include a Community Enterprise, Street Stewards and related projects. Every row of houses contains at least one Good Neighbour or Street Steward who can provide a range of activities – advice, parenting skills, first aid, safety, care for the elderly etc. In an area of, say, 5,000 dwellings and 15,000 residents there might be 60 streets.

If the Street Stewards of each set of 20 streets associate together to manage their own little task force of Caretaker and Health worker, a base and material resources, then wonders could be achieved. Thus, the whole neighbourhood might have 3 sets of staff each covering 20 streets and a co-ordinator, secretary and assistant to help the residents and their Capacity Builders to ensure effective delivery. The structure can be depicted and costed as follows:

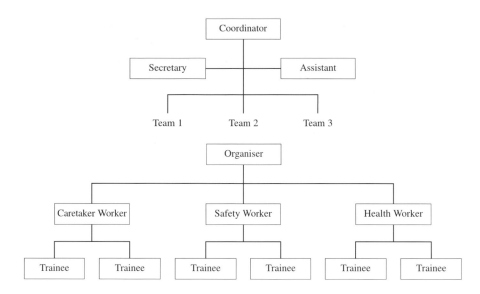

Figure 13: Chart of possible Community Team.

The Cost of these 3 coordinated teams might equal

Revenue

Co-ordinator & Assistant	At 25 + 20	£45k
Secretary	15	£15k
Organiser x 3	12	£36k
Caretaker Warden x 3	12	£36k
Safety x 3	12	£36k
Health x 3	12	£36k
Trainees x 60 running costs	15	£15k
	Total	**£239k**

Capital

x 3 Trucks	At 10	£30k

Summary of the above costs:

Capacity builder	203k
Neighbourhood Management	130k
Community enterprise	239k
Capital	30k
Total	**£602k**

Rather less than the £1,000,000 available from the neighbourhood budget!

Revenue total - £572k. Capital total £30k, Grand Total, £602k! This total still leaves aside £398k from the available £1m for special initiatives which will arise as the Neighbourhood's Development Plan is driven forward. Such a sum could fund a combined safety centre, health centre and Sure Start or it could fund a family centre in a school. Or, it could do all of these over a 3 year period.

In their powerfully argued book titled Neighbourhood Management, Anne Power and Emmet Bergin suggest that the costs of the staff needed to service each neighbourhood might be of the following order and that these could be funded from the housing budget alone. They are as follows:

For an area of 4,500 units as above

Function	Cost
Neighbourhood Manager	£60,000
Admin/PA	£18,000
Community support manager	£30,000
Admin/Organiser	£16,000
Supervision of environmental service delivery (2 posts)	£50,000
On-costs at 20%	£34,800
Super-caretaker/wardens (1 per 200 = supervisors – 24 post)	£480,000
Materials and equipment	£25,000
Office costs	£90,000
Community fund (£20 per household p.a)	£90,000
TOTAL	**£848,800**

Cost per unit = £189 annum; £76 per person

Figure 14: Budget for Neighbourhood Management.

From ideal model to the diversity of tailor-made provision

Not all neighbourhoods have 4.500 dwellings or 15,000 souls. Some have only 5,000, others have 20,000. So, some will command only 1/3 of the £1m budget. Others will have an additional 1/3. Similarly, not all will start with both the top-down co-ordination of services via a neighbourhood manager and the bottom-up capacity building of safety, environmental work and the street stewards described above.

Some will wish their neighbourhood forum to play more of a scrutiny role to ensure that Neighbourhood Management works and place less emphasis on the local provision of services by local people. Other neighbourhoods will, like LM schools, become semi-self governing and form alliances with similarly ambitious neighbourhoods.

So, there will be almost as many particular variations on the above theme as there are neighbourhoods. But, there are two common features. The culture must change from 'doing' and 'passive receipt' to 'enabling' and 'responsible activity' and very many more people will become involved in one or other aspect of the management and ownership of their neighbourhood. This ownership should not rest at social services but come to include physical assets.

The renewal of civil society and provision of enabling support for Active Citizens really does entail closing down our long established way of managing and funding care in the community and opening up under new, devolved, localised management.

Assets

The way we look after public land and buildings as well as services is vital. People, who own their own houses generally look after them, paint them every few years, repair the roof and replace the rotting fence. Local authorities are less good at looking after municipal housing. Castle Vale was a municipal estate in Birmingham's outer ring. Ten years ago it had almost as unenviable a reputation Balsall Heath. In 1996 a local Housing Action Trust (HAT) was given all of Castle Vale's municipal housing to manage. Previously, of course, it had been overseen from the centre of the city. As a consequence, we discovered in an earlier chapter, the feel and image of the neighbourhood has been so transformed that people even live longer and businesses which once would not have dreamed of investing in Castle Vale have now set up shop there and created local jobs.

In different parts of the country Tenants Management Organisations have had a similar effect. Residents in Royds in Bradford run their own business park and use a variety of assets to generate income which drives capacity building activities.

If 15 school governors can look after, manage and feel proud of their school and raise its standards, they and other local people can also own or manage such assets as these:

• Public housing
• Parks
• Small and medium sized patches of public land owned by various statutory bodies.
• Swimming baths and libraries
• Community and Leisure Centres
• Public buildings and land

Local communal ownership and/or management at neighbourhood level where real people live will inject the sense of pride which individual ownership involves. As a result, these assets will not become run down through poor maintenance and eventually require large sums of renovation money. Rather, they will be maintained and cared for.

Governance

Much of the case presented for the renewal of civil society in this book turns around creating a Commonwealth of semi-self-governing neighbourhoods in place of the existing Empires of urban authorities. It is possible to picture the governance of the neighbourhood and its relationship to the wider area and nation as follows in figure 15.

The reviving urban neighbourhood is a lively and active place. It might have a safety and health centre and its public spaces will become well used meeting places. Its parks are used and its school(s) might become community and family centres, perhaps also housing the urban village hall and the accessible office of the neighbourhood manager.

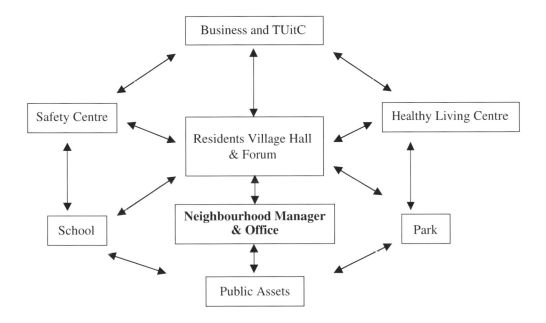

Figure 15: The Village Hall and its Neighbourhood Network of services & facilities.

The old top down culture looked like a pyramid sitting on top of a quiescent, atomised community. It departments and agencies operated in self-contained silos.

We are moving from that picture to something which resembles a maypole with each ribbon of the maypole representing a distinct neighbourhood. In place of Top-down silos will arise inter-agency, joined up, horizontal Neighbourhood Management teams or Neighbourhood Strategic Partnerships able to respond to the particular plan of the particular neighbourhood. They will look a little like this:

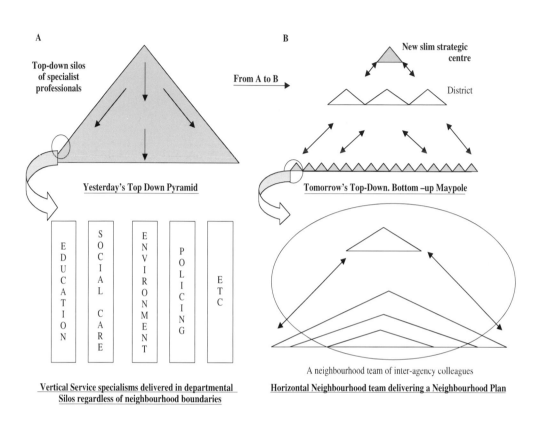

Figure 16: Picturing the future.

Chapter Six

REPLICATING SUCCESS – A LOCAL AND NATIONAL PROGRAMME OF CIVIL RENEWAL

A solution which will work and last is not yet in place. We have identified the problem facing the 3,000 excluded neighbourhoods as being social not material. In order to construct a solution we have explored the need to identify active citizens and build capacity and social capital in each neighbourhood from the bottom-up. We then argued that civil life in strong neighbourhoods needed to be complemented by renewed civic services, a neighbourhood budget, plan, team and manager. But, simply saying that this makes sense will not in itself produce the practical success we crave.

It is salutary to recall that 40 years of successive costly renewal initiatives have resulted in only a handful of success stories and that most of these triumphed despite, not because of, the system and its initiatives. As if in recognition of the desperation of this situation, in recent years two new costly initiatives were introduced. The first of these entailed 40 NDC areas being identified with each being given £50m over ten years. The second entailed 30 areas each being given some £7m to trial Neighbourhood Management practices, a total of 70 neighbourhoods out of the 3,000 ailing ones. A significant proportion of these struggle for the same reasons that prevented previous initiatives from working. But, even if they succeeded, it would bankrupt the Treasury to grant aid similar sums to even a fraction of the remaining 2,930 neighbourhoods. It is very clear that another way of turning fine words into replicated good practice is needed. Perhaps the secret of future success is to be found in those neighbourhoods which have already succeeded? Perhaps, that is, we do not need one more top-down initiative, however well defined, but one which arises naturally from the bottom-up?

In order to make progress each of the few recovering neighbourhoods has had to transform its image from 'bad' to 'good', from 'despair' to 'hope'.

To do this, each of them has had to engage in a variety of attention seeking exercises and to court publicity. It was not easy to get rid of the bad old image. So, the press, TV and variety of other ways had to be used of conveying to everyone both internally and externally that the old neighbourhood has been closed down and a new 'product' has been opened under new management which is attractive and welcoming.

An unintended, unexpected, consequence of this was that residents and professionals from other neighbourhoods – near and far- came to visit Castle Vale, Royds, Include, Balsall Heath Forum and others and asked: How did you do that? Can you show us how to follow suit?

It turns out that experienced residents who have succeeded in turning their neighbourhood round are very good indeed at explaining to less experienced residents and professionals how they too can succeed and provide them with the belief and courage to persist.

In the past, professional consultancies have made millions from trying to explain to others how to succeed, but have failed. It seems that residents are far better (and cheaper) at conveying to others just how to persist until they have succeeded.

Perhaps the idea of 'residents consultancies' and 'guide neighbourhoods' is all the better for not having been deliberately devised. It arose by happenchance. The idea was not created but was thrust upon succeeding neighbourhoods by residents and professionals who were eager to learn from them.

In the past, even costly government initiatives have been confined to a few areas. Neighbourhoods have had to compete for them. One has 'won', others have 'lost'. As the successful neighbourhoods were generally chosen by Local Authorities the decision was made on a 'buggins turn' basis and, invariably, the capacity of the neighbourhood had not previously been built, it was not already beginning to succeed. So, when the initiative ended, progress ended because local people could not sustain it.

Envisage, however, a rolling programme of neighbourhood renewal in which, say, 20 succeeding or 'guide' neighbourhoods are sponsored to help cooperate with and guide those that are not succeeding. Of course, at first each guide neighbourhood will only be able to help, say, 10 others with any degree of consistency and substance.

But, by this means, an ever-accelerating process of renewal can take place in what becomes a rolling programme of recovery. The initial 20 can each help 10 in year 1, making a total of 200. If by year two the 20 guides can each have identified just one more guide then they can have multiplied to become 40 each helping 10, making a total of 400. By this means within a 10-year period all 3,000 neighbourhoods could be reached. Of course, it would take all of these a further 10 to 20 years to have become fully sustainable. Yet, within 30 years, the task could be accomplished – a far, far, better outcome than the last 40 years and for a tiny fraction of the cost.

It is possible to picture the envisaged rolling programme in one urban authority as follows:

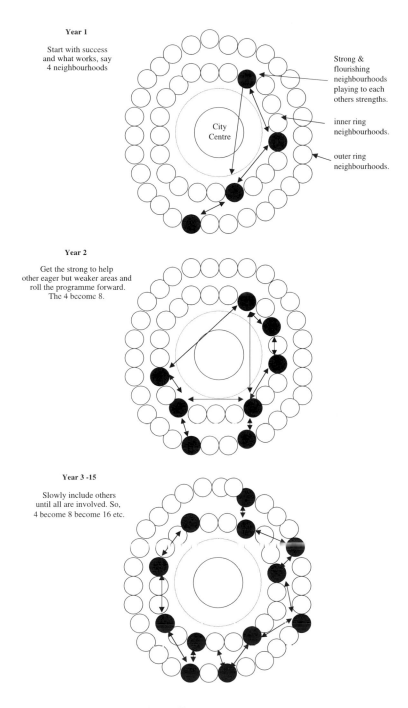

Year 1

Start with success
and what works, say
4 neighbourhoods

Strong &
flourishing
neighbourhoods
playing to each
others strengths.

City
Centre

inner ring
neighbourhoods.

outer ring
neighbourhoods.

Year 2

Get the strong to help
other eager but weaker areas and
roll the programme forward.
The 4 become 8.

Year 3 -15

Slowly include others
until all are involved. So,
4 become 8 become 16 etc.

Figure 17: Years 1, 2 and 3 of a rolling programme in one authority.

What defines and distinguishes a developed or Guide neighbourhood?

If we can be clear about what distinguishing characteristics an experienced or Guide Neighbourhood possesses, then it is both possible to recognise and accredit them and to show others the targets to which they might aspire. Characteristics might include:

- The process of resident led recovery has been underway for some years.
- The level of participation within local associations has risen markedly.
- Many people now feel confident and able to shape the quality of their lives.
- There are a growing number of resident led activities and voluntary associations.
- These associations have come together in some form of umbrella association, a Forum, Parish Council, Community Development Trust, Company Limited by Guarantee, a Charity or several of these.
- This association holds regular and annual meetings, and employs people to do a variety of tasks.
- These staff and their employers have a Neighbourhood Development Plan, parts of which they will deliver, other parts which will be delivered by a number of strategic statutory partners.
- There may be a Neighbourhood Manager and an inter-agency team of professionals working with the Manager, and the association of residents.
- Progress has been made towards improving one or more of these areas of life – the economy, education, safety, health, the environment, housing and the image of the area.
- There is determined local leadership and vision.
- The Local Authority and/or other statutory agencies are linked in productive partnership with the residents' forum and other local voluntary organisations.

Which Neighbourhoods are sufficiently advanced to be able to Guide others?

Castle Vale, once Birmingham's sick housing estate, now transformed. Today people live longer, are better educated and more people are in work. It is pioneering Neighbourhood Management practices.

The Eldonians redeveloped their own estate and provide a range of homegrown services.

Royds took ownership of an SRB programme and acquired land and property. Today they employ over 30 staff, run a variety of local projects and are fiercely proud of their achievements.

Balsall Heath was Birmingham's blighted red-light district. Today that is a thing of the past as residents support each other through 22 self-help associations. House prices have risen, people no longer wish to leave the area. Statutory partners help residents to implement and review a Neighbourhood Development Plan.

Bromley by Bow's transformation started in a run-down Church which now houses a nursery and craft activities. A park and Healthy Living Centre are amongst its achievements.

There are a number of other neighbourhoods such as Include in Liverpool and Poplar Harca in London which have also achieved remarkable successes. These include some but by no means all those which have received SRB, NDC and Neighbourhood Management Status. They and any other neighbourhoods which can fulfil the easily agreed set of accreditation requirements outlined above should be added to the list. But, at this stage in the recovery of the nation's 3,000+ neighbourhoods, no more than 20 can be said to be en-route to recovery, confident and capable of showing others the way forward.

Agencies which support Guide Neighbourhoods and residents
In addition to guide neighbourhoods, a range of agencies have arisen which are not geographically focused on just one neighbourhood. They cover wide areas, in some cases the whole nation. They serve a variety of individuals and groups in the community sector whose skills are of great value to Guide Neighbourhoods and those in need of support. For, they can teach Active Citizens the skills of Capacity Building. These include:

The Regen School provides training, advice and support for individual residents from an increasingly wide part of the country. The Regen school also offers capacity building for professionals.

Priory Estates Planning (PEP) provides a range of individual and group-training courses for tenants and residents. PEP also works out on location to help tenants and residents develop plans for their area. Like the Regen school, PEP also supports professionals.

Trafford Hall offers away-day courses for tenants, residents and professionals and can be booked by groups as a residential venue for training weekends and other events.

Regenerate provides a link between a number of Guide neighbourhoods and arranges exchange visits and advice for other neighbourhoods in need of their support and experience.

The Development Trust Association acts as the umbrella body for 300 plus Development Trusts and provides mutual support.

A number of other valuable support agencies such as Community Matters have arisen over the years which initially provided support for individuals and groups but which are now available to assist with the process of empowering residents in neighbourhoods. They should be added to the list.

Enabling Statutory Agencies

The 'doing', 'dependency', culture of statutory provision is in the process of changing to an 'enabling' and 'liberating' one. While there is still far to go, here and there key agencies and authorities have got ahead of the field and have become enlightened examples of good practice e.g. Wolverhampton where there are 7 neighbourhood management pilots.

These can be an invaluable support not just to Guides and Support agencies but colleagues in the statutory sector who are still struggling to find their feet in the new enabling culture as it emerges from the world of dependency. What will the best PCT, School, Police sub-station, Environmental or Leisure Services Department look like after some aspects of health care, policing, environmental maintenance etc are provided within neighbourhoods and what remains is brought to account by a Neighbourhood Manager working to a resident led neighbourhood plan? Those who can answer these questions will wish to aid those who can't yet do so in-order to assist Guide and Support agencies.

In mid 2004 the ODPM outlined what the best local authorities and LSP's (Local Strategic Partnerships) might look like in 10 years time. Incentives are needed to encourage those who move speedily towards this goal and sanctions for those who don't.

How have Guide Neighbourhoods, Support and Statutory Agencies operated so far?

Until recently Guide Neighbourhoods have concentrated on improving the quality of life in their own area. They have implied but not spelt out the answers to the big questions posed above. A few have helped adjacent neighbourhoods or ones in other parts of the country. Mostly this process of mutual help has been an ad-hoc one in which the Guide has responded to requests for help from visitors who had heard by chance of their success via one or more of a number of informal networks.

A very few Guide Neighbourhoods have set about helping others more deliberately. Balsall Heath's R4R network (Residents for Regeneration) and Bromley by Bow's CAN (Community Action Network) and those who have come together under the Regenerate project are examples of these.

There is a risk that Guide Neighbourhoods and Support Agencies and Authorities could continue to develop in an ad-hoc, uncoordinated, way. If so, progress will continue to be sporadic and slow. However, the time is ripe to bring

Guides and Support agencies together with best enabling practice within statutory services in a more co-ordinated way in a series of regional rolling programmes of neighbourhood renewal which combine to form a federal national programme.

Of course, each will retain its own unique identity and independence. But, it is time to advertise the services of Guides, Supporters and Enablers to a wider audience and consider ways by which more residents in more neighbourhoods can be empowered to play a fuller part in shaping their life chances.

The following scenario in each urban area can be envisaged:

- A typical urban area such as Sheffield, Bristol, Manchester or Birmingham might contain, say, a total of 60 neighbourhoods. Between ⅓ and ½ of these will be excluded and in need of renewal, say, 25. If just one or two Guide Neighbourhoods and a few Support Agencies can be identified in or near to such areas, they could start a rolling programme of renewal which aims to include all 25 excluded neighbourhoods within, say, a five year period.

- By this means, it should be possible to create a regional Rolling Programme of Neighbourhood Renewal within each of the 88 urban areas in which a Guide neighbourhood reaches out first to a few, then more and more less developed neighbourhoods. One or two of these might themselves presently become guides enabling still more excluded neighbourhoods to be helped until all 25 are included.

- The first 20 Guides, Support agencies & Enabling Authorities bear a heavy burden. They not only have to help themselves and others in their own urban area but others in urban areas where, at present, there are no equivalents. So, an all inclusive, well co-ordinated, National Rolling Programme made up of a series of regional rolling programmes will take some time to assemble. It might look like this:

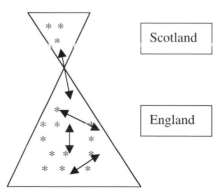

Figure 18. A network of regional rolling programmes.

Support for rolling programmes from HMG and LSPs

Guide Neighbourhoods, Support Agencies and Enabling Statutory agencies can start a series of rolling programmes. But, progress will be faster and more extensive if the enthusiastic support of Government and each authorities Local Strategic Partnership (LSP) can be guaranteed.

LSP were set up recently, given some funds (the Neighbourhood Renewal Fund) and tasked with devising strategies for community development. In addition, each of the 88 authorities was given an Empowerment Fund and was asked to use it to help create an empowerment networks so that Active Citizens could become more involved in the renewal process.

Fine words and intentions, but most LSP s struggle to turn these into good practice in real neighbourhoods. Again, when you think of it, it is surprising that no audit has been made in any urban area which could tell us with any accuracy which neighbourhoods are succeeding, which are failing, which are in transition from one to the other, which have access to and use guides and which lack or possess Capacity Building facilities. Many don't even know how many neighbourhoods they have.

With the help of their Empowerment Network each LSP could undertake this auditing task. Paul Slatter, Director of Birmingham's Empowerment Network has suggested that each might be able to produce a chart of the neighbourhoods within their catchments area. It might look like this:

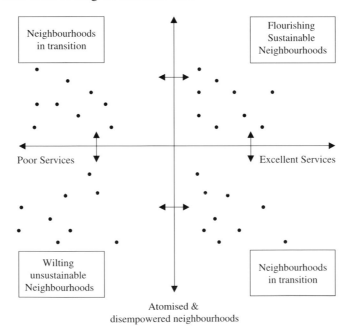

Figure 19: Chart of different types of neighbourhoods.

We really do need to know what is being done to identify which neighbourhoods are failing, what is being done to help them to succeed and what targets and timescales are being set. Some service deliverers have inspectors who check the quality of that service and suggest ways of improving it. Where necessary, they issue warnings. Schools, for example, have Ofsted, the Office for the guaranteeing of standards in education.

Perhaps this is the moment to remind ourselves about what our bank manager would say if we went to him for a loan for our neighbourhood if he knew that it was a £100m a year business which had no manager, no business plan and a poor product.

As neighbourhoods don't have bank managers, perhaps they should have an equivalent of Ofsted, an Ofsthood? Rather than invent a whole new inspectorate, it would make sense to ask LSP's and Empowerment Networks to act in this way and start by doing the audit of neighbourhoods suggested above. Clearer instructions should be given by Ministers to LSPs to undertake such functions as follow with the promise that they will continue to receive their Neighbourhood Renewal Fund if they comply and the threat of withholding it if they fail to do so:

- LSP's to identify, support and use succeeding or guide neighbourhoods to start a series of rolling programmes of recovery.

- LSP's to reduce the number of failing neighbourhoods in their catchment area year on year and to aim to have no failing neighbourhoods within 15 years.

- LSP's to use the NRF only for the renewal of neighbourhoods and not topping up mainstream funds or for one-off projects.

- LSP's to have the power to put a seriously failing neighbourhood into a school's equivalent of 'special measures' and not let it out until it can demonstrate that it is en route to recovery.

It would concentrate the minds of LSP's if a handful of them were found wanting by their Government office and their NRF was withdrawn until they demonstrated the clear will to act as proposed. Too drastic? Not a bit of it, especially if you are one of the thousands of people resident in that area, let alone a taxpayer. Ofsted can remove a school's governing body or its head and pull in a successful head to sort the situation out. Surely, LSP's (or someone) should have similar powers in cases where a whole neighbourhood is failing and a variety of services are inadequate or can't perform well enough because of the social context in which they have to operate?

Hitherto, we have chosen a very few failing and unprepared neighbourhoods to 'win' scarce but substantial grant aid in competition with others who 'fail'. The 'winner' has invariably used the money to top up already failing but costly services. The 'losers' have assumed they can't progress, as they received no support.

In place of this approach, Government is advised to choose to reward the few succeeding neighbourhoods in return for them not competing but cooperating with weaker ones with the active blessing of their LSP. Thus, with the judicious use of the stick of sanctions and the carrot of praise, it should at last be possible to make real progress. We are in need of a far bolder, concerted, coordinated approach if we are to tackle the huge problem we face. But, one crucial ingredient in the recipe for success has not yet been discussed, the relationship between Participatory and Representative democracy.

Chapter Seven

CONNECTING PARTICIPATORY DEMOCRACY WITH THE REPRESENTATIVE KIND

The Active Citizens, Strong Neighbourhoods, Neighbourhoods Management and the Rolling Programmes of Neighbourhood Renewal advocated above have significant implications for the way we view representative democracy and the public sector. Too often, the politicians and officers who staff Central and local government and other statutory agencies behave as if there were only two sectors in society, their own public sector and the private sector.

Yet, there are, of course, three sectors, the other being civil society, the third or voluntary sector, the realm of the Active Citizen. All three sectors are equally important for the functioning of the wider society. But, the balance between them can become distorted to their own individual detriment and to that of society as a whole.

Indeed, throughout the whole of the last century the role, power and effect of the public sector steadily grew as the Welfare State was constructed while the role of civil society shrank. The former has become too strong, the latter too weak and the relationship between them became distorted and, unbalanced. This, in part, is what has created the hole in the social ozone layer and this is what makes it so difficult for excluded neighbourhoods to become sustainably renewed.

This is the problem which Active Citizens have identified and struggle against the odds to solve. Yet, understandably, even many enlightened influential public sector figures don't see this problem or that they are inadvertently contributing to it. The culture is changing – slowly. May have begun to adopt the language of devolution and localisation. They are beginning to 'talk the talk'. But when you look at the way they 'walk the walk', the good language masks old habits which die hard.

As recently as mid 2004 the ODPM published 'A prospectus..' for Local Area Agreements and 'The future of local Government: Developing a 10 year vision.' Both documents were designed to show that Local Government must reform and that we must focus on building sustainable neighbourhoods. Yet, when they refer to 'local' and 'community' they invariably confuse these with the 'Local Authority' and 'representative democracy.' They talk of elected Councillors being 'community leaders' and assume that they will chart the way forward for neighbourhoods which struggle, not the active citizens in civil society who live in these neighbourhoods.

These are major errors of judgement which will slow, not hasten, recovery. The solution requires the very clear recognition of the difference between the public sector, representative democracy, and civil society, which is the realm of participatory democracy and a rebalancing of the relationship between the two sectors so that it is productive, not damaging.

The credibility gap between the people and the politicians who have provided the one-size-fits- all services of the Welfare State has become worrying large, especially at the level of local government. So, the implications of new, resilient, neighbourhoods for the strengthening of the democratic process are potentially important. Is it possible that civil renewal can help civic renewal and that the gap between them can be bridged?

Progress can only be made if we admit that the representative way by which the existing system of welfare is held to account has become as inadequate to today's world as the industrial mine and cotton mill of yesteryear. It is now out of synchronisation with where people are and what urban regeneration requires. It can't deliver what people yearn for – a better, inclusive, life for their children. Alone, it can't make neighbourhoods safer, healthier, cleaner, greener and more generous.

Representative Democracy

Today, representative democracy gives all over the age of 18 the vote. The vote is exercised once a year in local Council elections when the voter elects one of three Councillors for a three year period and once every five years in General Elections when an MP is elected.

This right to vote for a person who is invariably from a political party and who will represent the voter for 3-5 years, was hard won. Women had to chain themselves to railings and go to prison to achieve it. People who did not own property had to campaign for it. More recently, the vote was given to all 18 year olds. So, representative democracy has evolved and changed. It is still changing. Soon, the first past the post system may be reformed to make way for proportional representation.

Representative democracy is good. It was a very great advance on what went before when only one powerful land owning aristocratic class had access to power and the levers of government.

But, it also has its draw-backs, especially in today's age of instant communication where the voter knows as much, if not more, than the politician, where ordinary people are no longer happy to accept state provided one-size-fits-all services because they have learned from the manufacturing world the virtues of choice and diversity and the power they can command over the quality of what is on offer.

The Draw Backs

Each Local Council ward has a voting population of about 25,000 people and a population of 40,000 plus. A Parliamentary Constituency can contain 65,000 voters and 90,000 people. Respectively, what do the voters do for the next three and five years after they have elected their representative? Politically and practically speaking, they do nothing. Further, voters do not select the politicians who they can vote for. They are chosen by party activists of whom there are very few. So, voters can't vote for whom they choose. Their choice is limited to one of three or so people who were selected by the few activists and perhaps a few minority party candidates.

No wonder that, in some areas, less than 20% of the voters vote in local elections (59% in the last general one). Of these, up to 50% plus vote for the candidate(s) who is (are) not selected. So, less than 10% of the electorate vote for the person who is elected. That is, 90% plus do not get the person they want! This country, in particular it's inner and outer city areas, compares very unfavourably with others. See figure 20 below.

Turnout in Recent Local Elections Across Europe

Luxembourg	93%
Sweden	90%
Italy	85%
Belgium	80%
Denmark	80%
Germany	72%
France	70%
Spain	64%
Ireland	62%
Portugal	60%
Netherlands	54%
Poland	43%
U.K	40%
Walsall M.B.C	25%
Many Inner and Outer City Neighbourhoods	18%

Figure 20: Turnout in Recent Local Elections

Once elected, Councillors then go to the Town Hall to manage the large bureaucracies of City Departments and follow their party line. MPs do likewise in Whitehall. The effect that either has over the voter's home, family, street, park, school, job is minimal. Their contact with the voters or their neighbourhood between elections is non-existent.

Yet, we now have more Councillors and MPs and the Town Hall and Whitehall are now larger than when the country governed 50% of the whole world 100 years ago.

"In political terms, the creation of the Welfare State saw the triumph of representative democracy over civic democracy in personal welfare, housing, education, health and the general environment." In other words, Frank Prochaska argues in the IEA's publication, Involuntary Action, the Welfare State represented "the triumph of the national community over the local. It was in keeping with the trend in which central governments eliminated or sidelined the pluralistic traditions of voluntary institutions. Greater government control and the principle of universalism brought undoubted benefits, but with the result that citizens became consumers of government rather than its producers. Paradoxically, individuals were in some ways more impotent in an age of universal suffrage and parliamentary democracy than the disenfranchised had been under an oligarchy in the past."

The outcome of representative democracy can thus be summarised as follows:

- **Poor services** that do not relate either to the individual or to the neighbourhood they live in.

- **Apathy** about representative democracy whose hard won history is fading from the collective memory.

- **Disrespect** for the politician and politician parties. Their popular rating is lower than that of the used car salesman.

- **Danger,** for the credibility gap between those who represent and those who are represented is wide and widening.

This is sad, for many politicians are good, hardworking and caring people. But, we must conclude that representative democracy has gone just about as far as it can go before it must make a further quantum leap in its evolution if it is again to become valued and respected. This unsatisfactory situation can be summarised in chart form:

The Nature of the old Local Authority	The consequence for the neighbourhood
Budgets were administered centrally. These funded services are throughout a local authority's whole territory.	Neither local people nor officers nor Councillors knew what those services cost each agency; let alone what the cost of all services was in each particular neighbourhood.
The Local Authority used to set its own budgets to deliver / provide services throughout its domain with no regard to the boundaries of the neighbourhood which were contained within it.	Residents played no part at all in delivering services or assisting with the management or government of the neighbourhood. They certainly had no funds or budget of their own.
The Local Authority was concerned with the inputs it made into the whole urban area it covered. But, while it paid great attention to expenditure, tracking and administering its budgets correctly, it was not interested in the outputs, the effect of these on people in neighbourhoods.	The outputs of City funded and supplied services are registered in neighbourhoods as being consistently poor - low educational standards, high crime, etc. All people could do in response was register dismay or anger.
Councillors commanded and set policy. Officers administered it. Officers felt responsible upwards to councillors and not downwards to the neighbourhoods in which the outputs of their actions were experienced by residents.	Residents played no part at all in shaping policy, services and outputs, except for the 20 per cent of adults who vote once a year in elections, They felt powerless and excluded.
Local Authority services were one-size-fits-all monopolies. No diversity or choice was offered. The initial instinct of old style MPs, Councillors and Officers who wanted to solve the problem of Neighbourhoods of Despair, which their old-style organisation had helped to create, was to throw more money at them. This only made the inputs bigger and the outcomes worse. It wasted money. It did not solve the problem.	The only way any resident could exercise a choice for themselves was if they could muster the finances and effort to move to a 'better' neighbourhood elsewhere. The unheard, unregistered cry from the heart of residents in Neighbourhoods of Despair was: • "Please do better than this." • "We know what we want, but we don't know how to achieve it." • "Give us the knowledge and resources and we will find a way." • "We are excluded from the political process."

Figure 21: Representative Democracy – as it currently exists.

Participatory Democracy

Civil Renewal, Capacity Building and the new ways of managing neighbourhoods described earlier represent a very different kind of accountability. It's called participatory democracy.

The object of the exercise of participatory democracy is not to involve people in just one vote once every few years but, to get as many people as possible to be actively engaged as citizens each and every week, to create and sustain networks, associations and to build and sustain strong and resourceful neighbourhoods.

People of all parties and non-party members are engaged in participatory democracy, the more the better. There is scope and space for everyone. Indeed, the ultimate aim of the successful Capacity Builder is to engage the entire community and exclude only the criminal and the anti-social neighbour.

Party politics does not enter into participatory democracy. Indeed, it will only succeed in involving most people if it is non-party political. The only issues it is concerned with are these:

- How can we all combine to keep the streets safe, the environment green and welcome newcomers?
- How can we help schools to raise standards and use their premises to aid community activities?
- How can we engage local young people, provide them with good role models and gainful employment?
- Etc

The only time when voting for one person or another might arise is to decide who is best suited to represent their neighbours on a Council or Police Committee or to judge which 10-20 people are most able to form their Neighbourhood Forum. But people will not vote for those who stand because of some political consideration. The questions in the mind of the voters will be these: Who is most energetic? Who is most consistent? Who is good with words and persuasive?

Further, once elected, such representatives will not disappear into some remote chamber. They report back to their neighbours at regular intervals about what they are doing. And, because they live in the neighbourhood they serve, their ear is always close to the ground.

At first, those engaged in participatory democracy will remain diffident and unsure. They will feel inferior to officers, experts and Councillors and unsure about how to deal with them. However, as time goes on and they become more practiced, experienced and certain, they will feel able to enter into robust partnerships with them and to advise them about the best way forward for their neighbourhood. If the experience of the few recovering neighbourhoods is anything to go by two important developments will follow.

First, more and more residents will see the point and purpose of voting in Council and Parliamentary elections. In place of alienation and apathy, enthusiasm will arise as people see how they can make an impact on the system and gain a degree of control over the representative model.

Second, some of the more active residents in the more active neighbourhoods will conclude that they can do at least as good a job as existing Councillors and M.Ps and, maybe, an even better one. Some will join one or other of the parties. Others are likely to stand as independent resident candidates.

One of the aims of the Balsall Heath Forum is to double the number of people voting in local elections. If this aim can be achieved and replicated in other neighbourhoods, this could be just the breath of fresh air which stagnant Representative Democracy needs. Participatory Democracy, could be the saving of it.

The liberation and logic of the Private Sector

We now know that it is not possible to try to rationally order and arrange the whole of society via the state from Whitehall and the Town Hall. Or, if we do, disaster will eventually result.

The change in culture and attitude required to recognise this was first won in relation to the Private Sector. The left's attempt to nationalise the commanding heights of the economy led to the Winter of Discontent and an ailing economy. By degrees, we realised that the last mechanism we needed to drive the economy was a committee of elected politicians. Instead, we needed an entrepreneur who would be judged not by an annual vote but by customers and by shareholders with a stake in the company which the entrepreneur created.

That argument is now largely won, not just in this country, but in the whole of the developed world. Even Russia and the East European states, once communist, now know that to compete with the West they must become fleet of foot and mind if they are to offer their customers not a camel but a horse.

Civil Society – the Third Sector

However, too many politicians still believe that their public sector should command and 'do' things for the third sector or civil society because ordinary people are not able to do things for themselves.

As we have seen, this admirable intention – to help people – had an unintended and highly debilitating consequence. It made people dependent, robbed them of initiative, self-reliance and the capacity to help themselves.

The gradual nationalisation of the way we care for each other by the public sector must now be reversed. However, this is the very opposite of the privatisation which some on the left instinctively believe it to be. Rather, it is mutualism.

Once known, long-forgotten, Lessons from the 1800's
Members of the Labour Party who feel their existing vocabulary of class and conflict and equality does not yet match the growth points of the freshly emerging, morally driven, relations between the private, public and third sectors may find some comfort in looking farther back in history than the collectivism of the state which has dominated the twentieth century.

The Chartists and Co-operators practised ethical socialism in the 1800's and built the first Trades Unions. Robert Owen didn't try to take control of the state to legislate for schools for all. He built schools with and for those who attended his factories. In those days, ethical socialists didn't wait for others to do things for them. They created an astonishing array of thriving local associations, which gave meaning and value to their families and neighbours. This was not an uncaring or selfish individualism. It was at one and the same time both individual and human-scale neighbourly mutual care.

Friendly societies arose later in the nineteenth century. Working people contributed gladly to them knowing that those who fell upon hard times would be helped. They employed their own administrators and doctors. By the end of that century 7,000,000 people belonged to a friendly society.

In those nineteenth century days, it would have been difficult to predict that the twentieth century would see the rise of the Welfare State. For, may people envisaged that the Friendly Societies and Mutual Associations would develop their role of providing assistance for people who became sick or unemployed or old. Powerful arguments were, therefore, developed in those days to show that 'progress' would consist of increased wages for working people so that they could contribute more of their earnings to their Friendly Society so that it could provide a greater range of Welfare Services.

In Friendly Societies, rights and responsibilities were intertwined and freely given. People supported each other. If the state was allowed to take on this function then, it was supposed, ordinary people would loose the ability to help each other. Thus, it would no longer be necessary for people to exercise responsibility. The state would do it for them and this, people thought, was wrong and diminishing. Rights and responsibilities would become separated and opposed to each other. The quality of life would suffer. Deja vu!

In addition to the prophets, the chartists, co-operators and mutualists have all taught us that people are individuals. Yet, they can only express their individuality and become fully human in a family, collective, communal and moral setting. Individualism and collectivism are not, as the political parties would have us believe, incompatible opposites, they are essentially the flip side of the same human coin. At different times in history, however, one side of this coin has been emphasised by philosophers and politicians to the detriment of the other. This has resulted in discordant social relations, a divided and uneasy society.

The development of an approach which combines the virtues of both collectivist and individualistic ways of organising social affairs could mark the end of a period of major debate and conflict between those who argued for a caring public state and those who have advocated private initiative. We stand at the dawn of a new era. In place of the public control and uniformity of the industrial era and the Welfare State we are about to experience:

- A renaissance of communal enterprise, self-help and the building of substantial social capital, of participatory democracy.

- A remodelling of the public sector so that it enables and does not provide or diminish, of representative democracy.

- Moving from a Welfare State to a Welfare Society.

Capacity Builders, Entrepreneurial Managers and the new Town Hall

Although it is relatively novel to the urban scene, the active citizen's neighbourhood forum, their Capacity Builder and those local voluntary and non-government institutions which relate and are accountable to them do not comprise an additional layer of government, which further complicates the organisation of the democratic process. Rather, they take the place of significant parts of the previously over-intrusive Council machine. As a consequence, the Town Hall can concentrate less on trying to run everything and thus failing to do anything well, but like any enlightened manager, on enabling and resourcing others to achieve excellence. Because so many of the tasks once undertaken by the Town Hall can readily and more effectively be discharged within each urban village neighbourhood it is necessary to reduce its size and change the way it is organised. Most of the Town Hall's vertically organised, top – down, departments can be slimmed down or merged in order to meet the new horizontal functions of the kind which neighbourhoods really need. Having lost the control and management of 'their' schools to school governors, a number of authorities have closed down their education committees. Kirklees has done this as has Calderale, Rotherham, Barnsley, Gateshead, Hammersmith, Brighton, Hove and Fulham. Once an authority has also let go of all its houses and some of its other services it will need to rethink its whole point and purpose. The local authority of tomorrow will look very different from that of today.

It follows that a fresh, community-sensitive, Council department is needed which cuts horizontally across the Local Authorities old vertically designed bureaucratic and professional specialisms. This new department might subtend an array of sub-departments, one for each neighbourhood. These neighbourhood sub-departments would marshal and deploy the levers of local government to service and enhance the growth points of each neighbourhood. The old and new roles of councillors and participating Active Citizens can be illustrated in another chart, as followers:

New Style Councillors	Neighbourhood Stewards
Do less, enable more and provide vision for a whole urban area.	Do more in their own neighbourhood.
Are not threatened by new developments but help their old-style, top-down, departments to find new ways of working horizontally at neighbourhood level.	Respond and form good working partnerships with new style representative councillors.
Are paid as if they were professionals because they have become professional managers in charge of the devolution of huge budgets of taxpayers money and are responsible for the inspectors of outputs.	Are, like old-style Councillors, unpaid people who put in a substantial voluntary effort.
Are already recognised as competent to take decisions which not only affect neighbourhoods but whole Local Authority areas. Nonetheless, training is needed if they are to manage new style City Departments, Neighbourhood Managers and Neighbourhood Officers.	Require support and training to build their capacity to influence local events. Just as the newly forming Trades Unions movement needed to found Ruskin College and run 'workers' Education courses to enable its shop stewards to become more effective, so also street stewards who are helping people in the neighbourhood to organise their affairs, need a Community College.

Figure 22: New Partners in Participation.

These roles are not entirely new. Many towns have developed neighbourhood offices in recent years, though not always in response to a clear neighbourhood voice. The Capacity Builder and Neighbourhood Forums can provide that voice. They can be the locally accountable body to which city government devolves funds and functions.

Because the aim of this new department is to boost the confidence and capacity of the individual, see to it that others assist the developing child and take part in the revitalisation of neighbourhoods it could be called the Neighbourhood Enterprise Department. Once this new department is devolved out to area officers in each neighbourhood it, in effect, becomes their new mini-or Neighbourhood Town Hall.

Its staff will be joined by officers from the police, primary care group and representatives from the private sector in the Senior Neighbourhood Managers inter-agency team. Together they will work with the Neighbourhood Forum and its staff to devise and deliver the Neighbourhood's Development Plan.

The Neighbourhood's Town Hall becomes the new Local Authority's devolved top-down lever with which other statutory agencies and the Neighbourhood Forum liase. It might be based in an extension of one of the neighbourhood's schools or in its village hall thus becoming one of its finest and most valued local features.

Far from there being the need to worry about the 'democratic deficit' the devolution of services to neighbourhood teams and the community creates a substantial 'democratic advantage'. A start has been made. Birmingham has created 11 Districts, each with a District Committee, Director and staff services devolved from the centre. Leicester created 9, Liverpool 7. Those are all moves in the right direction. But Sandwell has created not District but Neighbourhood teams. Wolverhampton is experimenting with 7 neighbourhood management pilots.

It is as difficult for those who have been used to doing things centrally to devolve right down to the grass roots as it was for LEA's to give up their power and budgets and transfer these to each school with its own set of Governors. But, unless this challenging step is taken, civil renewal will not take place because residents will neither own nor sustain it. So, it is important to see that the devolution underway in Birmingham and various other authorities is only the start of an evolving process which will eventually transfer power and budgets from the centre through Districts to the real neighbourhoods where people live.

The problem is not unique to this country. In 2000 AD. Robert Putnam wrote "Bowling Alone" in which he detailed that more and more Americans participate in fewer and fewer communal activities. Today, he said, "They even go bowling alone". This seemingly small phenomenon is echoed in many features of social life which cumulatively have serious implications for the quality of life in neighbourhoods and adversely affects people's health and happiness. His identification of the problem and his proposed solutions struck a chord with thinkers on both sides of the Atlantic, in part, because he pointed out that Americans had faced and solved a similar problem 100 years ago.

A new role for local authority
Territorial nationalism is becoming weaker. In the European world of postindustrial technology and instant communication, nationalism fades in the face of the global village. At once, power moves up and away from the borders of this country to

Brussels and worldwide markets and, at the same time, it is shifting down to the urban village, street corner, family and individual.

In the new world of the new millennium the grip of the national politician and the industrially shaped political party will become even more tenuous while the role of the urban authority and the previously ordinary, inconsequential, citizen will become more and more significant.

It is in this context that the radical reform of the old-style Local Authority does not, as some supposed the Conservative government's reform of the '80's intended, imply its abolition. Rather, it suggests the development of a highly effective new kind of local government. One of the major roles of this new authority will be to create the neighbourhood-specific devolved department described above. There is, however, a range of other tasks which can only be discharged from an over-arching local authority civic centre. These include:

- The allocation of budgets between neighbourhoods, although this can be done by means of a nationally agreed, value-added, formula.
- Responsibility for the dissemination of best practice between neighbourhoods, the inspection of the performance and services of mini-Town Halls and Neighbourhood Managers and the application of sanctions if agreed targets are not met.
- Performance management. Just as there is the need to close the failing school, sack the head and re-open it under new management, so there is the need to do the same with failing neighbourhoods where officers from pre-existing departmental silos fail to play as a team.
- Responsibility for transport policy in association with regional and central authorities.
- The oversight of refuse collection and disposal.
- Planning decisions when these impact beyond the confines of any one neighbourhood.
- The branding and marketing of their urban area to the nation, Europe and the global village.

However, there is no reason why the elected local authority councillors and their slimmed down and redrawn departments should themselves perform any of these functions. Rather, it is merely essential that they ensure that some competent body is contracted to undertake them. The councillor's role is that of the conductor of the orchestra, and not that of the many instrumentalists of the orchestra itself.

This change has already taken place in the case of Local Education Authorities where such functions as inspection, careers advice, are provided by a new breed of independent educational enterprise. It is similarly to be expected that some of the functions which Local Authorities have undertaken will, in future, be discharged by:

- Neighbourhood Forums themselves or clusters of them.
- Community Development Trusts and other self-governing local agencies.
- Independent suppliers in the private sector.
- Consortia of these.

In additional to devolving many of its old functions and budgets to neighbourhood level and checking that the desired targets and outcomes are achieved, there is one crucial central function which will grow.

The old, industrial, function of towns which drew agricultural labour from the green fields to staff the urban factory's workbench has long gone. The new high-tech industries, commerce and tourism, are the means by which new economic purpose is being given to urban areas by businesses and local authorities working in partnership. If these partnerships do not blossom, some towns may never acquire a new purpose. Like the 'ghost town' of the spaghetti Western film they may die.

Regardless of Whitehall those that do flourish are likely to build upon their regional, national and international connections, become more like city-states and less dependent on the nation state. As these modern towns develop new functions the role of the City-Centre Manager will become more and more important. Only 10 years ago there were just 4 such managers. Now there are over 200, all working to turn around the faded image of their town or city centre and develop it into a vibrant one with the help of private and public sector initiatives.

There is much interesting talk of rediscovering a national identity and of re-branding Britain. But the need to perform this service for towns and cities is of paramount importance if they are to develop a new post-industrial role. Neither the private nor public sector alone can achieve this. Imaginative new initiatives are called for and many exciting examples are now to be found in different urban areas, which owe nothing to the politics of the past and everything to Councillors and City Officers who have helped their town or city to find a new purpose and pride. Birmingham's image was of metal bashing and Spaghetti junction. Today, it is of canals, the International Convention Centre, the NEC, and a World Class Symphony Orchestra. It is twinned not with London but with major European Cities. It has offices in Brussels and Chicago. And, at home, it has meetings with Bristol, Manchester, Sheffield and Nottingham in an alliance, which could come to overshadow the importance of the one it has with the capital.

The newly emerging role of the Representative Local Authority and the Participatory neighbourhood is summarised in figure 23.

Authority	Neighbourhood
Does less itself and enables people in neighbourhoods to do more.	Stops grumbling that the Authority isn't solving its problem and takes local action to solve them.
Changes its political and planning lines to coincide with these of socially/ geographically defined neighbourhoods.	Appoints a Social Entrepreneur or Forum officer whose task is help local people to form new local associations and a Neighbourhood Forum
Appoints a Civic Entrepreneur as a Neighbourhood Manager with a small team of interdependent officers whose task is to target inputs so as to achieve outputs agreed with the community.	Draws up a Neighbourhood Development Plan and costs it.
Negotiates the cost of all the Neighbourhood Development Plans in its area, divides and devolves its budget between these neighbourhoods.	Implements its plan and reviews it year on year. Implementation includes each neighbourhood in: • Providing some services itself • Buying in others from elsewhere e.g other neighbourhoods, and the private sector as well as the Local Authority
Commissions each neighbourhood to deliver its plan.	Revise targets in line with inspections of its outputs.
Agrees a set of standards to be achieved in each neighbourhood, then inspects to ensure the agree targets/ outputs are met.	The neighbourhood gains choice, diversity and the services and outputs it wants and the sense of responsibility, inclusion and pride
The local Authority gains respect and the satisfaction of its customers.	Neighbourhoods are the basic building blocks which the wider City 'neighbourhood of neighbourhoods' is built. They form an active, two way, relationship with it.

contin...

A number of functions remain. These include services which only the Local Authority can accept responsibility for and deliver or commission because they affect all neighbourhoods. Examples includes:

- Developing and marketing a vision for the town/ city centre and for the town city as a whole.
- Transportation policy.
- Inspection of the quality of services in neighbourhoods.
- Regeneration to government.
- Representation to Europe and other towns and cities.

They assert and develop their own image and style. They welcome newcomers and stronger neighbourhoods help weaker ones.

Figure 23: Radical reform = Hope.

Representative Democracy will govern with the help of a Cabinet of Senior Councillors who will champion new departments ranging from the one which markets their urban areas nationally and internationally to that which empowers and enables the many neighbourhoods within its boundaries to find their identities and deliver their own self-help services.

Just in case anyone supposes that the 'remaining' democratically elected Councillors are being demoted and will have little to do, the very opposite is the case. Each neighbourhood will need an elected representative champion who will present the needs of its participatory Forum, Senior Manager and Trust to the Cabinet. Hitherto, local Councillors have been the very opposite of local. Once elected, they have disappeared into the corridors of power in the Town Hall and have had no visible local effect other than to become the backbench voting fodder of their party's kitchen cabinets. In future, it will be important for them to become a respected local figure who is applauded for gaining and using the resources their neighbourhood needs to build its capacity and deliver its neighbourhood plan. This will, of course, entail redrawing local political boundaries so that they coincide with neighbourhood ones. Again, the changes entailed are considerable and will take several years to achieve.

The great Victorian Town Halls which symbolised municipal splendour at home while Britain's Empire expanded abroad have become decaying monuments to a past era. Yet, while cotton mills and docks have been closed and reopened as offices and museums and business has adopted a new style of devolved organisation, the multi-million pound organisations of local government still hanker for past security and are often an impediment to growth. If more of them do not also move with the times and find a fresh way of catching the voters' imagination their future will be in doubt and the worrying credibility gap, which the opening paragraphs of this chapter described, will continue to widen.

So, although the reforms proposed are radical and require dramatic changes in style, attitude and outcome, they represent no more of an attack upon local government or the Welfare State than John Harvey Jones' attempts to save fading industrial businesses by importing information technology and rethinking the way they are managed signify an attack upon them. On the contrary, the reforms could rescue the political process from decades of inertia and popular resentment and herald a new era of acceptance, appreciation and vigorous growth. Thus, one key indicator of a thriving participatory neighbourhood and successful renewal is if the vote for representatives goes up dramatically, not down.

Chapter Eight

REKINDLING MORAL
AUTHORITY – LOCALLY

What drives and motivates the active citizen? What binds them and their neighbours together in strong communities? What enables Active Citizens in strong communities to join in partnership with their statutory partners yet retain their independence? The answer has to be – shared subjective values and people with emotional maturity who possess the authority needed to uphold these values.

Yet, in today's world, shared values and respect for authority are in short supply, particularly in the 3,000 excluded neighbourhoods which cause us most concern. So, ways of developing and asserting moral authority must be found.

- **Academic, Social and Emotional Intelligence**

School is now compulsory for all children from the age of 5 to 16. Further, more and more children aged 2, 3 and 4 go to pre school nurseries and other establishments. More and more aged 16 to 21 also go to sixth form college, college and university.

So, our society is good and getting better at educating and refining the academic intelligence of young people, in part because our economy needs brighter and brighter brains to ensure that it competes successfully with others at an international and global level. Yet, we are far less good at developing their social and emotional intelligence.

Citizenship is now taught as a part of the national curriculum. While this means that young people know something of our unwritten constitution, fewer and fewer say they are interested in the political process or see the point of voting. Teaching citizenship by the blackboard is very difficult. It needs to be taught 'by doing' but we are not very good at the practice of it.

We are even worse at the practice of emotional intelligence, the kind which makes us socially sensitive and aware, alert to other people's needs and feelings as well as our own, able to encourage and support others and show the skills of leadership needed to maximise the potential of friends, neighbours and whole communities – and raise the next generation with refined and loving parenting skills.

Emotional intelligence used to be taught unwittingly in the home not just by parents, but grandparents, other relatives, the church and wider community. But, as these traditional tutors of emotional and social intelligence faltered, no modern institution has arisen to take their place.

So, if civil society in neighbourhoods is to become united, strong and respected, the Capacity Builder and Active Citizen will have to construct commonly agree values and find ways of authoritatively asserting and sustaining them. This chapter discusses some of the practical ways by which this can be done in each neighbourhood. The next chapter describes the support which local people will need from national leaders if we are to fill the vacuum.

First, we need to remember that social life really can't be governed by relativity. It does need to be guided by common rules if it is to be cohesive and people are to respect each other. A glance in turn at football, the classroom and parenting will remind us of this enduring truth.

- **Football, or any sport**

The game of football follows a series of rules. Each team is only allowed 1 goal keeper, 11 players in all. There are a host of codes which tell players what to do when a goal is scored, the ball goes into touch, a player is off-side etc.

Further, a referee is needed to remind the players of the rules. If a player ignores them, the referee shows them a warning yellow card and, if necessary, shows them a red one and sends them off the pitch. Follow the rules, obey the referee and the game dances and delights. Flout the rules, ignore the referee and the game collapses into chaos and someone will walk off with the ball in a sulk.

- **Teaching a class of children**

Any school also needs a set of rules and a timetable. For, unless class 'A' are in room '1' when their teacher arrives to teach them maths, they do not learn.

We all know that although the rules of a school are important, on their own they are not sufficient. Like the referee, the teacher must be a figure of authority and impose their personal authority or the naughty boy at the back of the class will soon make all 30 pupils un-teachable.

- **A parent**

Many of today's young parents have learned to be too indulgent of their children. They try to be their friend as well as their parent although their child needs to look up to a figure of love and of authority. Too many of today's parents enter into a kind of conspiracy of immaturity with their children.

Yet, indulge and give in to the temper tantrum and any successful parent knows that you build up more and more serious behaviour problems for tomorrow. On the contrary, 'be cruel to be kind' and the child learns to respect both the parent and themselves.

Every child will test the rules to discover where the lines in the sand are. Give a little and fine, you have gained the respect of the child! Give a lot and the child is soon uncontrolled and that respect has been lost.

It is possible to provide common sense example after example, which shows why we need both agreed rules and authority figures, the referees, who are needed to impose and uphold them. But, we must stop and say: Its just the same with life in neighbourhoods and in the wider society.

Neighbourhoods and society will only be calm, cohesive, loving and supportive of children and adults if they have common values, a morality, a set of rules which people agree to abide by and a structure of authority, leaders, who impose the rules, teach and, if questioned too loudly, have the moral courage to send the offender off the social pitch.

The creation & celebration of communal morality

A few more stories from Balsall Heath might set the imagination going about how we can create rules, identify referees and an authority and set of values in any neighbourhood.

•   Carnival

In the midsummer of 1973 a few residents were firmly advised not to organize a Carnival in Balsall Heath. "Nobody will come," it was said. "They'll be too frightened and the experience of failure will be worse than no experience at all". The residents were told by Council officials: "You must not try to raise expectations. They'll only be dashed and we'll be blamed all over again for the state the place is in. Don't do it"

The officials could have turned out to be right. Gangs of teenage boys roamed the streets and were used as apprentice drug runners and pimps by more hardened criminals. People were afraid to go out at night or to use the local park. Perhaps people really would not come. Indeed, most people simply did not suppose it was possible to hold a successful communal event which would not get disrupted by gangs of disrespectful youths.

A few residents met and discussed whether to go ahead or not. Ted, a Trades Unionist now long dead, said: "If we give in to the fear of failure we'll never progress. It's like organising a picket." He said: "If your workmates don't believe you have the courage to win a concession, they won't join you. There's strength in unity." He added: "But unity doesn't come without example. My wife and I will bake some cakes and we'll sell them on a cake stall." So, against the odds, Balsall Heath's first carnival for forty years took place in 1971.

There were a dozen stalls, of which Ted's was one. There was dancing from one of the local primary schools, singing from a gospel choir and other special events. Just four lorries were dressed up as floats and the organiser made sure that the local police were a very visible presence. Just 300 people came. They had a pleasant afternoon. All the cakes from the cake stall were sold and several people said: "Make sure you do it again next year and make it bigger and better." They also said: "And see to it that the police are around again." Six male officers had patrolled the event and, in a nearby road, a police van was visibly present with another dozen officers ready for action.

Fast forward over the next 30 years, which brings us up to today. During each of these years a carnival has taken place. Each year it became easier to organize as confidence grew and residents re-discovered their streets and took ownership of their park and leisure pursuits. In 2004, the Carnival attracted 5,000 residents in family groups. There were 80 stalls, 20 floats and special events. But, there was just one police officer who herself staffed a stall recruiting special constables from members of a community which had once, quite literally, been at daggers drawn with those in authority. Renewal takes time. It takes persistence. It takes authority.

- **Balsall Heath in Bloom**

For some years now, the Carnival has featured a 'garden of the year' competition as today's organisers salute the effort which residents have made to turn the Balsall Heath of the bleak and bad old days into a beautiful neighbourhood.

This gave residents the idea of entering Balsall Heath into the Midland's Regional section of the national Britain in Bloom competition. Recapturing and planting derelict land, reclaiming parks and placing planters along the high street led the neighbourhood first to come third, then second, then first in the Midland's section. This put Balsall Heath through to the National finals. It came runner up and the neighbourhood was filmed by BBC TV and featured in Gardener's World alongside far more affluent areas.

Astonishingly, letters of congratulations arrived from Scotland, Wales, Devon, Middlesbrough and London's East End. These letters also asked: "How did you do that? Our neighbourhood is a bit like yours. Can you show us how to do likewise?"

People know what they want, a better life for their children than they have experienced for themselves. But, they are not sure how to achieve it. Show them the route forward, give them the resources and they will rise to the challenge. Joe, Balsall Heath's Head Gardener picked up a chip packet thrown from a car window. He handed it back through the window saying: "I think you dropped this." He got a lot of abuse. He pointed to a bin a few yards away. The abuse continued. By then several residents had gathered. They took up Joe's cause. "We are tidying these streets. Stop it," they said. The driver said "sorry" and left.

- **Street Stewards**

Street Stewards are men and women, young and old, black and white who act as active and caring citizens. The reader will recall that every street in Balsall Heath now has at least one. Some have several. They are the modern equivalent of yesterday's good neighbour and they have a little of the village elder or priest about them. But, they had to be found, introduced, given the courage of their convictions and, where appropriate, training and support.

They have become the backbone of their street's residents group, given it substance and continuity. They are the ones to whom residents turn for the phone number of the police or rubbish removal squad, who identify a neighbour in need of help or who is becoming a nuisance. They welcome newcomers, and let people know when the next public event is to be held and they help to distribute the local newspaper.

Alongside schools and faith groups, they are the new fabric of the community. They hold it together. They give it substance. They are its glue. They are its authority. And, they are organised, encouraged and inspired by Gloria who, the reader will recall once wanted to move because she feared for the safety of her young family.

• **Christmas parcels**

Last Christmas, the Community Wardens were concerned about a number of elderly folk who lived on their own. To be lonely and on your own at Christmas is one of the worst experiences. It is depressing and sad. So, some of the Neighbourhood Forum staff went to the four primary schools in the neighbourhood, spoke at their assemblies and said: "Think about it. Lots of people will be on their own and won't have much fun. But, you will. For you, Christmas will be warm and full of life and you'll be opening presents from your family. So, why not bring in an apple or pear or tin of fruit or biscuits and write a card."

The children and staff made over 200 food hampers each complete with its card saying: "I love you and I'm thinking about you at this festive time." They put on Santa Clause hats and delivered them on Christmas Eve and Christmas day. There wasn't a dry eye in the place. And, of course, it wasn't so much the hamper, which went down well as the thought. It really did count. It made a lot of people feel very good. – including the staff who said: "They all appreciated it so much. I feel terrific." Truly, to give and to receive are their own reward.

• **The Walking Bus**

They say imitation is the sincerest form of flattery. Balsall Heath's Neighbourhood Wardens borrowed the idea of a walking bus from Castle Vale.

Too many children are driven to and from school when they could walk. So, the Wardens started at one end of the neighbourhood and weaved their way to school past dozens of children's homes. Each day they deliver 36 children to school early where they have a good breakfast and enjoy each other's company. It makes them fitter, healthier, punctual and ready for a good day's work.

If the young, why not also the elderly many of whom felt fearful on pension day of walking on their own to the post office? So, now they too form a walking a bus accompanied by the Warden as 'driver' and 'ticket collector'. It's not just the sense of safety which is important. It's also the company, the chat with the warden and the fact that they can also mention other things which concern them.

I was taken aback one day when talking to two pensioners. When asked about the Wardens they said: "What Wardens? What are they?" I explained: "Oh", they responded. "Why didn't you say, the men in green". The Wardens wear a green uniform and are known locally as 'the men in green'. "I'd trust them with anything", one said. "I've got their mobile number and I can phone them any time about anything. They're always popping in for a chat and a laugh".

• A community newspaper

While Balsall Heath gets a good press today, many years ago it did not. The commercial press only printed the bad news. Thus, to highlight the good news, one voluntary organisation decided to create a local newspaper. Balsall Heath's 'Heathan Newspaper' started many years ago as a single duplicated sheet. Today, it comes out every month, is delivered through every letter box in Balsall Heath and is a glossy and professional product which prints not just the good news, but passes on useful phone numbers, exhorts local agencies on towards greater and greater feats and identifies issues for the authorities to tackle.

The Balsall Heath neighbourhood 'printing press' now issues not just a Neighbourhood Newspaper but a neighbourhood calendar and lays out the annual reports of local agencies in an attractive way, which makes them readable and reassuring.

• The Balsall Heath Honours

Some people are just naturally good. They give without counting the cost to themselves. Nationally, such people are honoured by the Queen and made an MBE, OBE or whatever.

Long ago, Balsall Heathans decided that a local Neighbourhood Honour was also needed. Every so often a ceremony is held in which the local lollipop lady, street steward, good neighbour or activist is recognised and applauded in front of their peers and given a 'Balsall Heath Honour' for good citizenship by the Lord Mayor or some other dignitary. The scroll they receive is worth its weight in gold. So, also, is the fact that they become a role model for the young in place of yesterday's pimp and prostitute.

• Raja, the Trades Unionist

The reader will recall that Raja organised the pickets who took to the street corners to shoo away the kerb crawlers and end street corner prostitution. The pimps were furious. Their lucrative business was threatened.

One accosted Raja outside his house. He said: "I know where you live. I know your wife and children, and I know you." Raja invited him to look up and down the road. By every other house stood a resident. Raja said: "Feel free. Harm me and one of them will take my place and we all know where you live. So, why don't you go?"

Pause. Silence. Raja stood his ground. The pimp turned and left. He did not return. Facing down the neighbourhood bully takes real moral courage. And, it was the making of a new kind of authority in Balsall Heath which resulted in the grateful kiss of the young mother described in chapter 1.

• V.I.P. visits

Everyone responds to a pat on the back when someone in authority says: "Well done." Balsall Heathans have met a number of V.I.P.'s. They have been congratulated by David Willets and Oliver Letwin who said: "I truly admire what you have done." A couple of Labour stalwarts had to stifle beams of pride. Lord Ashdown came when still plain Paddy and said: "You have achieved wonders." The same stalwarts beamed their beam and shook his hand.

David Blunkett has visited several times and now knows some key residents like Gloria personally. Most recently he was garlanded by Mary Beasley from her wheel chair before 300 cheering residents. He said: "You are the proof that recovery is possible. You are a beacon illuminating the way for others." This time it was the turn of the local Conservatives candidate for a Council seat to smile and shout 'bravo'.

But the wildest cheers were left for Prince Charles who has also visited several times in his capacity as President of Business in the Community. He met those who had most recently been honoured, moved from table to table crammed with people who had made a difference and said: "You are a place of all faiths and one community. You are the future for this country." People of all parties and all faiths and none were delighted. It was true reward for all their hard won achievements. Reward too for the fact that dozens of people had litter-picked the whole neighbourhood the night before, placed bunting along the main streets and erected welcome signs on the key entry and exit routes.

• Persistence

The congregation for the Christingle service in St Paul's Church in the heart of Balsall Heath in 1971 was made up of just six people. The heart and soul really had left the body of the neighbourhood to rot. There was no hinterland, no authority.

The first meeting of the first residents group attracted 3 residents. Now 24 groups meet regularly. On average, 23 residents attend each of these. Thus, 552 residents now meet every month or two to discuss practical and even more important issues.

Soon the Neighbourhood Forum will gain its 1000th member. This is the 'village Council' which elects 18 residents to represent them and employs a team of staff who work with them to make the area safe, clean, green and spirited and join with statutory agencies to make services better and raise standards.

Once, officials said that local people were unemployable and that it was far too risky to give them resources or enable them to take part in the governance of their neighbourhood. There have been many ups and downs and disasters on the way, But, today, the modern equivalent of these officials are trained by residents and their staff who are beginning to show them how the other 90 plus neighbourhoods of Birmingham can be made to flourish. If Balsall Heathans can do this, so can people in any neighbourhood in the land.

• **Assemblies and meals**

A school has an assembly most mornings to bring the school community together. A church or Mosque has a congregation which worships together every Sunday or Friday and is united in common belief and concern.

In Balsall Heath those of all faiths and none join the Neighbourhood Forum. Members have rights and duties. It holds an annual meeting when written and financial reports are given and new members are elected to the governing executive committee. But, this only happens after a buffet meal has been served to the 300 plus people who attend. There is music, displays and stories of success and kindness are told.

People who have come from the 4 corners of the earth sit together, eat, share their stories and discuss what they aim to achieve over the next 12 months. Mothers bring their children. Street Stewards bring their new neighbours. It's an indoor equivalent of the outdoor carnival. It is the neighbourhood's equivalent of a church communion.

• **Faith Establishments**

Balsall Heath is fortunate to now possess three Mosques, two Sikh Temples, a Synagogue, five Churches and a significant minority of the population who attend one or other of these. Even though the part which religion plays in modern life is on the wane, faith establishments and their leaders can play a significant part in the renewal of civil society if they will consider not just their own believers, but look to the common interests of the wider community.

So, an inter-faith 'tent' has been pitched which aims to introduce the faiths to each other, foster mutual understanding and discuss the common ways by which the faiths can help ordinary residents to acknowledge their duty to help and support one-another in sickness and in health regardless of their particular belief.

• **Leadership**

There is a saying: "One citizen defending his home is more powerful than ten hired hands." That is why, at the end of the day, every Empire there ever was has disintegrated as people with local affections and identities assert them in the face of distant authority. So, it is with people in neighbourhoods. But they need to be organized and they need to be well led.

Try to imagine a football team without a captain or school which did not have a head-teacher. Or, a church which did not have a vicar. Or, a firm which did not have an executive director. Most neighbourhoods have come to have no head, vicar or leader. So, little wonder that they have floundered as the objective, rational, centralised state tried to take the place of the local leader and displace the local, subjective, authority.

In times past, much of the civil life of families and neighbourhoods was organized within the parish boundary of a church. The priest would lead the members of the parish in prayer, baptise, marry and bury them, visit and minister to the weak and mark the seasons with special services at Easter, Harvest time and Christmas as stories were told which gave life common meaning. The Church was, quite literally, the life and soul of the place, the glue which held it together and saw it through bad times and good.

This kind of parish has long gone as has its priest. It is not only not possible to return to those days, but it would be foolish to try. However, the function of caring for people, their need for communion with each other and being united by a common view remains as urgent today as then – more so, because of the confusing, rudderless, space which now exists in place of point and purpose.

It is common sense really. Of course, a neighbourhood needs social leadership which will bring its residents together in some shape or form. In some places that leadership might still come from a person of faith or a head teacher who sees the need for their school to be surrounded and supported by a vibrant neighbourhood. In others, it will be some modern equivalent of a Parish Council, a Neighbourhood Forum, with an elected executive.

There is no one-size-fits-all. Each neighbourhood will devise its own tailor-made solution. But, it is certain that each neighbourhood does need to devise that solution, then bind it into the fabric of its being.

The tide is turning

Every so often the tide turns. In place of swimming against the tide, you suddenly feel that it flows with you. The tide has turned. A new situation has arisen in Balsall Heath. Again, if it can turn in Balsall Heath, it can turn anywhere in the land – with the right resources and leadership. But, good, active, people in the 3,000 excluded neighbourhoods of the land which lack cohesion and a commonly agreed code of conduct will be aided if, in addition to doing such things as are described in this chapter, they are helped by the nation's leaders.

Chapter Nine

REKINDLING MORAL AUTHORITY – NATIONALLY

If we expect values and authority to be asserted from the Bottom-up alone by Active Citizens and Capacity builders without help from national leaders from the Top-down we will be waiting a long time for success. Even then, it will be sporadic and many areas will remain bleak, unorganised and disintegrated. Universal success will depend on a concerted national effort which supports and encourages the efforts of leaders at the local level.

Renewing the culture - The identity of place and the Rites of Passage
We need to be taught by our national leaders that:

- When the child is young and vulnerable its parent(s) and the wider local community should swear an oath of duty to care for, feed and look after them.

- This oath should include putting so much back into the environment of the place where the child grows up that he/she feels proud and safe in it.

- As each subsequent stage in the child's growth is passed, the child/adolescent/ adult must return that care and mark it by also swearing an oath, so that in place of just receiving they also begin to give and recognise that by the end of their life they must have put back more into the community than they have been given by it.

- Such things need to be taught in the home, in the community and in the school. Indeed, they should be taught in the way people live, not just in lessons in school but in the way the school and community are organised and the informal and formal codes by which social life is ordered and organised. They are, in effect, the 'standing orders' of life. They are the rites of passage.

Get the local culture right and the national culture will follow
Get the body language of the child-in-their-neighbourhood of origin right and we have the foundation upon which to build the common sense of citizenship.

That is, having been cared for as a child, it becomes entirely reasonable that the adolescent should graduate from school by agreeing to invest their talents and ability to care for others back into their community and town.

Beyond that, upon reaching the age of 18, when the child is granted the adult right to vote etc, the new adult should inherit the responsibility to support the wider nation.

Without this local-leading-on-to-national inheritance, the forces of law and order are powerless and James Bulger and Damilola Taylor will result again and again.

Every society known to mankind has had to create its own version of the above. The stages and rites of passage have always been marked by elders with ceremonies and customs which have become woven into the tapestry and story of life.

In the case of our society, this tapestry of tradition has become faded and torn by the pace of change. It is no longer strong enough in the urban village for ordinary folk to hold onto. So, it is time that the elders or leaders of our nation – not just politicians, but people of faith, those in a position of communal leadership and parents – discuss how to weave a fresh tapestry appropriate to the changed circumstances of our modern age. Then, they need to impose it with authority and leadership.

Rights and responsibilities spelled out

Younger countries than ours, such as Canada, as well as older Eastern ones can teach us how to do this and contribute to our debate. Our rites of passage, our induction and acceptance into adult maturity evolved and were passed on by custom and word of mouth in an unwritten constitution. Now that this glue has warn thin, we have nothing in writing to fall back on which might tell us what to do.

Canada had no traditions and customs and so had to write things down and make some formal agreements to help its diverse people to stick together and respect each other. We should study its experience. Perhaps we should agree a few simple basic responsibilities which could be matched with rights and written in a freshly agreed list such as follows:

Rights given to the individual by Community & Country	Responsibility to Community and Country of the individual
Child Benefit	Caring for and teaching your own (& other) children to respect themselves,
Free Schooling	each other and the law of the land
Access to the NHS	Contributing to the health of the community, caring for its environment and being a good neighbour

contin...

Safety from crime	Reporting crime and serving on a jury
Social Security and other benefits	Paying taxes
Freedom of speech & information	Allegiance to Queen and country
The vote	Participating in communal affairs

Figure 24: Rights and responsibilities.

A new year of Community Service

Once the list has been more elegantly and simply crafted, how might we present it to every young person in the land upon reaching, say, the age of 18? Until relatively recently every young man had to do two years of National Service in the armed forces. Many benefited, especially youngsters from difficult backgrounds who gained an education and character building. So, the Nation also benefited.

In this day and age, young men and women would all benefit from a well organised, robust, year of Community Service which might be seen as a direct, if practical, part of their education, one specifically oriented to the arts, practices and values of emotional and social maturity, of citizenship.

Too many of us might still blink at the idea of making this year of communal service compulsory. So, perhaps it should at first be voluntary, but made more exciting by a number of incentives which might make it tomorrow's version of today's 'gap year.' It might count towards an NVQ, Degree and other certificates. Those undertaking it might get a 50% reduction on the repayment of their student loan or be paid a citizen's wage for the year if the person concerned is not intending to go to college.

Couldn't, shouldn't, the Home Office's Active Communities and Civil Renewal Units and the DfES be charged with organising this year? It may, of course, cost them a bob or two. But, the civil renewal benefits would render it cheap at the price.

On February 18th 2004, the Chancellor spoke to a conference of the National Council of Voluntary Organisations and suggested that 'a call to service among young people' might become the norm. Ruth Fox and Thieu Besslink (Connecting People, the Fabian Society, 2004) wrote that 'such a clarion call to service for young people across the U.K would be a seminal moment in our history. It would indeed.

Having learned about 'citizenship' in theory as part of the national curriculum in schools young people would learn about the institutions of civic society and develop a sense of trust in each other and the organisations they serve through their year of community service in society. A wide range of community service placements might be considered, such as these:

- Working in a voluntary or community organisation.
- Teaching primary age children to read or mentoring a difficult pupil.
- Working in conservation and environmental placements.
- Working in a hospital or with social services.
- Working with a faith group.
- Community service overseas in troubled countries.

There is the prospect of a veritable army of young people who could, if well organized, accomplish a great range of socially valuable tasks which would not otherwise be undertaken. In the process, they would become better citizens able to steward social life as aware, concerned, adults.

The Graduation Ceremony

Passage from the practical School of Community Service warrants a Graduation Ceremony and the presentation of a Certificate which enshrines the Citizen's Rights and Responsibilities and surrounds and celebrates it with a fair bit of pomp and circumstance.

Newcomers from elsewhere now have to undergo an induction ceremony into the citizenship of this country. That's fine. But, shouldn't every person, including all those born here as well as newcomers, have to undergo a 'rite of passage' signifying their inclusion into adult citizenship? Shouldn't everyone have to go through this special graduation ceremony, accept the rights and, in return, swear to undertake the concomitant responsibilities which the year is intended to instil and explain? The ceremony might take the form of a school prize giving ceremony combined with the atmosphere of a community carnival or celebratory meal.

The Queen Mother's funeral, the Golden Jubilee celebrations and our victory in the Rugby World Cup reminded us all that we can be quite good at enjoying ourselves and engaging in a bit of Midsummer Night Revelry. The ceremony should be full of fun as well as gravity.

So, the celebration of each and every person's Graduation into Adult Citizenship should become the most noteworthy of the rights of passage, a cause not just of a communal celebration within a neighbourhood but of a national one.

Some 80 years ago, the 11th hour of the 11th day of the 11th month became first Armistice, then Remembrance Day. Everyone now stops for a moment at that time each year and Whitehall and the Cenotaph host a special event to honour those who gave their lives so that others might live.

As our unwritten constitution evolves and we slow the pace of change to capture the concept of our mutual interdependence and emphasise the duty of the young to their community and country, couldn't we have an annual Day of Duty of which all in that year who Graduate into Adult Citizenship are honoured, perhaps at a ceremony of Youthful Maturity to be lead by a 'Prince of all the Faiths,' but not a politician. With the help of schools and faith leaders and community capacity builders, this could put pride into people, their neighbourhood, their city and their country.

While Politicians could encourage debate aimed at such an outcome, they couldn't possibly lead it unless they were not just agreed but enthusiastically united in a cause which was above and beyond party interest. They would need the keen support of all key players – faith and school and community leaders.

They would need to see that this was at once intended as a lasting epitaph to Damilola Taylor, James Bulger, Steven Lawrence, Holly and Jessica and an acknowledgment by us all that if the Queen can: 'Vow to Thee my Country", then so can each and everyone of us, in a Day of Duty and a Celebration of Commitment to others which binds us all together in Civil Society.

Jonathan Sacks, the Chief Rabbi, reminds us that the key word in biblical ethics is 'covenant'. In a covenant, "parties come together to pledge themselves to a code of mutual loyalty and protection. Like a contract, a covenant is born in the recognition that no individual can achieve his or her ends in isolation. Because we are different, we each have strengths that others need, and weaknesses that others can remedy. Unlike a contract, however, a covenant is more than a narrow legal agreement bound by mutual interest. It involves a commitment to go beyond the letter of the law, and to sustain the relationship even at times when it seems to go against one's personal interest. A covenant is an agreement in which higher moral force, traditionally God, is either a direct party to or guarantor of a particular relationship. The idea of covenant reminds us that there are some rules whose claim upon us are stronger than short-term self-interest and involves a commitment to the institutions into which we were born and from which our identify derives."

A movement to renew the social environment

In place of strife and political discord, something of a non-and all party and all-faith movement is emerging. After arising as a fringe concern, followed by a long period of both national and local discussion, most people now accept that the physical environment of the earth cannot indefinitely absorb the post enlightenment outputs of unrestrained scientific and industrial progress – excavations, emissions, pollution and toxic wastes – without serious damage being done to the land, sea and air. The environmentalists have shown us over the last 30 years that without links being made between personal responsibility and the common good the planet will be destroyed. Therefore, we are all beginning to apply the principles of stewardship to the natural environmental so as to conserve it for the benefit of future generations. We all now worry about and seek to repair the hole in the ozone layer.

The same principles are now being applied to the social terrain. It is becoming increasingly clear that the foundations and guiding axioms of social and cultural life also do not have an infinite capacity to withstand the erosion which results from 'taking out more than is put back in.' As with the earth, social life in developed countries like modern Britain has also been ravaged to such as extent by the age of industry, its organisational structures and concepts, that it has become impossible to maintain a civilised life in key parts of the nation. So, the task of each succeeding generation must now be to steward society and leave the quality of social and cultural life, as well as the natural environment, in a better condition than when they found it.

In times past, change was so slow that the torn fabric of the community would be refurbished without many people having to think or act overtly about it. It just happened with the helping hand of grand-parent, doctor, priest and squire. Today, it will not. As a whole nation we all now need to consciously invest time and resources to discover and apply the best means of replenishing and sustaining community at the levels of family and local neighbourhood as well as in the wider society.

As with environmental stewards, the work of Active Citizens, Capacity Builders, Civic Entrepreneurs and Street Stewards was at first isolated and unrecognised. They swam against the tide. They did not figure on the agenda of politicians. Now, a sea change is taking place.

Changing the culture – Who can do what?

To find the will to create and sustain Civil Renewal and create a new Welfare Society in place of a Welfare State all hands must be challenged to play their full part, in ways such as these:

The state, central and local can:

*   Recognise the general problem and that the state itself became part of the problem because it came to do too much and has intruded too far into the communal sector, weakened its resolve and made it dependent.

    Thus, like the Empire, it needs to withdraw from the Commonwealth of the communal sector in a phased way while enabling and funding it so that it can do more. It needs to fund Capacity Builders and Social Entrepreneurs and the local associations they create.

    This will entail switching its renewal programmes into being people and not property and project led. It needs to turn them into Rolling Programmes of recovery in which the strong help the weak.

    In particular, this means not just bending mainstream budgets, but finding very different ways of managing them so that people in communities have the resources and assets needed to deliver many of the services once provided for them by the state.

The ODPM and the Home Office's ACU and Civil Renewal Unit, aided by Regional Offices should scrutinise every Central and Local Government policy and ask: Does it help to create a cohesive, stronger community/neighbourhood or not? How can this and other policies be made to have a more positive effect? A more strategic, less doing, state and a more authoritative and resilient community entails the need for a new compact or partnership between citizen and state.

We have argued that Local Authorities should restructure and create a new department of neighbourhood renewal as it devolves services and responsibilities to a lower level. To symbolise the new covenant, Central Government should do likewise.

One Ministry of State should take a leading role and spearhead the changes and proposals outlined in this book and which will arise from the national debate about civil renewal. The different bits of different Departments concerned with renewal should be brought together, probably under the guiding hand of the Active Communities Directorate to give them single minded focus with the leadership of Minister of Cabinet rank.

Political Parties can:

• Contend with each other not to search for each other's weak spot and create conflict, but to play to each other's strengths and build a more consensual and enabling approach to what needs to be done.

Schools, Colleges and Universities can:

• Play a hugely important role in developing children and families and their parents views of citizenship and the way we must care for and respect each other.
• Ensure the new year of civic duty is well organised, attractive to most and a highly valued component of each person's CV.
• Teach us all to understand and respect the Cathedral of Civilisation whilst also showing us how we can add to and develop it.
• Help us to respect science and pure reason, but place them within the wider context of the subjective value and quality of life.

The faiths can:

• Look beyond their immediate followers and set an example in the neighbourhoods where they are based.

- Revisit 'Faith in the City' and update it in an inter-faith exercise.
- Train priests in the skills and techniques of renewal and social entrepreneurship and make appointments with care.
- Talk to each other more and play an increased, mutually supporting, role within the neighbourhoods in which they are based and in their governance.
- Demonstrate to us that the traditions and values of the newcomer from the East have much to teach the West and that, far from being a problem, they are part of the solution for which the whole nation yearns.

The voluntary sector can:

- Redouble its effort and recognise that it has a leading role to play in renewing social life.
- Prepare to take on the challenge of delivering more services from within the community.
- Support an army of Capacity Builders, assist with their training and ensure they are supplied with the resources they need.
- Connect with and lead the Rolling Programmes of Neighbourhood Renewal.
- Demonstrate that Representative Democracy can only thrive if it is counterbalanced by strong Participatory Democracy.
- Work as one with Faith Establishments.

The private sector:

- BitC, Business in the Community, has a large role to play in putting back the things which its members have taken out of communities and in showing both state and community how to be more enterprising.
- So too has TUitC, Trades Unionism in the Community. Today, we need to help people to organise in the places where they live, not just in the places where they work. The principles of organisation used by Trades Unionists in the places where people work should be applied to the creation of decent conditions in the places where they live and to raising the quality of life in excluded neighbourhoods.

Together, the state, faiths, voluntary and private sectors can:

- Initiate and sustain not just action, but a series of regional debates about the need to mend the hole in the social ozone layer and create sustainable Civil Renewal. These should feed into a National Debate or Conversation about the needs of civil society and the way we must care for each other. While the State could play a significant part in facilitating this debate, it should be led by leaders of all the faiths, BitC, TUitC and the voluntary sector.

- The conversation should be sustained over a lengthy period and aim to reach a Tipping Point where the cultural tide turns, attitudes change and a new balance or covenant is reached between the community and other sectors of society.
- We have had an Urban Summit. We now need a Social Summit – located every year in a different region - until we have understood the threat to the foundations of the Cathedral of Civilization and the depth of the hole in the social ozone layer and learned how to mainstream the former and diminish the latter.
- Flowing from this national and regional conversation will come a variety of practical and symbolic initiatives, such as:
- Introducing a new kind of National or Communal Service for all 18 year olds.
- Expecting those who move from adolescence to adulthood to pass a rite of passage which includes induction into adult citizenship in a public graduation ceremony.
- Initiating an annual national Day of Duty.

Previous top down renewal initiatives have been property led and time-limited. Perhaps we are now clearer that successful, sustainable, renewal has to be people led and part of an on-going process. If it is to be people led and practiced in every excluded neighbourhood in the land, then it requires us to look at the apparently dated concept of subjective authority with fresh eyes and grow it anew – from both the local and the national levels.

Chapter Ten

FROM OLD LEFT AND RIGHT TO A THIRD WAY

Identifying the hole in the social ozone layer, stewarding our inherited social cathedral, encouraging Active Citizens by Capacity Building, creating voluntary organizations, managing and funding neighbourhoods differently, asserting common values and leadership have clear implications not just for a new relationship between participatory and representative democracy but also for the ideologies and theories of the political parties.

All the ingredients needed to renew civil society in the many excluded neighbourhoods of the land have now been outlined and their interdependent nature discussed – with one exception. The culture of politics, the way we envisage society and how it can be changed is the one major factor yet to be considered.

Facing this factor will require real statesmanship from politicians, their parties, advisors and an ability to stand back from their short-term party political interest and take a detached, long term, view which is in the broader interests of society as a whole.

For a very long time, a major fault line has run through our politician's culture and, thus, the way those who lead and staff the political and public services think. It is long standing, deep rooted, and makes it difficult for them to see clearly the need for the radical reform of the services which they have grown accustomed to delivering. Hitherto, it has been possible to avoid recognising that serious flaws exist in the nature of service delivery simply because they don't have enough money. If only we can redistribute mere wealth, politicians have believed, services will improve. Yet, 40 years of costly renewal initiatives have not touched the problem. The excuse wears thin.

However, it is difficult to persuade those who are caught up in delivery to accept that they are part of the problem when, for 150 years, they have thought that they were part of the solution. It is only human of them to find it difficult to agree that they are mistaken and that the foundation upon which they stand is built on sand, that the route they have taken is one of societies cul-de-sacs.

Since the days of Karl Marx in the mid eighteen hundreds, socialists have tried to extend the notion of collective self help from the working class work place and mutual society to the state in both economic and social affairs. One hundred and fifty years later, we now know that this theoretically derived attempt to manage the economy and run industry by bureaucratic, collective, planning simply did not work in practice. The individual entrepreneur, responsible to his/her shareholders, and the rigueur's of the market place have proved to be a far more enduring and effective way of producing and delivering a range of goods from which the customers can chose than the one-size-fits-all variety delivered by the collective state bureaucrat.

We tried very hard and for a very long time to make the latter work in both Eastern Europe and the West. But, it simply, and quite literally, did not deliver the goods. Thus, it has fallen by the wayside except in the practice and minds of a few who still cling to the once exhilarating, now fading, dream. They still yearn for the success of public, collective, production and mistrust, even despise, the private sector entrepreneur and their independent creation of economic capital.

Little wonder, therefore, that they find it almost impossibly difficult to apply the lessons of failure in economic life to a similar failure in social life. For, they can't see that the way we have 'nationalised' the way we care for each other and delivered one-size-fits-all social services in education, housing, environment, leisure and safety have also failed to work. Indeed, it has failed very badly indeed, particularly for all those who live in the 3,000 excluded neighbourhoods of the nation.

The old Polish and African story about how to feed a hungry person reveals the fault in previous thinking and points the way forward. It tells us that we simply should not try to do things 'for' people, to give them a fish, for it withers their sense of responsibility and confidence. They loose their sense of independence. They will not identify with or sustain what has been done. It also wastes resources. On the contrary, do things with people and 'enable' them to fish for themselves and it generates self-reliance and dignity. And, they will care for and sustain what they have produced. Whatever funds have been used in the process will have been well spent. They will have been an investment, not a grant.

The failure of 'collective sate socialism' gave some Conservative thinkers hope. Having 'defeated' collective thinking in the economic sphere, they began to wonder if they could do so in the public, social, arena and, thus, privatise the caring services.

Yet, the social market works by quite different axioms from the private market. Unlike the customer, who seeks to buy a new T.V or fridge, the resident who wants a good park, school, environment and the sense of safety can't shop around and choose between different products. Merely, they want a better product, a more effective way of delivering it and a say over the quality and maintenance of it. They don't want a choice between different kinds of fish, just the right to make their own rod and fish with it in their own pond.

This does not mean that all residents in all neighbourhoods have to provide everything for themselves. Far from it. But it does mean that the collective state itself should not always provide services for them, even at a local level.

So, its not the case that we need alternative parks or schools or environments from which we can choose, but alternative ways of managing the one local school, park and environment that we have in each neighbourhood. If such facilities are not to be managed centrally by the collective local authority, who can do it? There are a variety of alternatives to choose from which have been discussed in earlier chapters. They include:

- Residents might do it for themselves.
- The Neighbourhood Manager and their neighbourhood team.
- Once the local school has mastered the intricacies of its own management, is there any reason why it should not also look after the adjacent park or leisure centre if it wants to?
- Or, it could be the local housing association, HAT or TMO which might be driven to also look after the environment, service the neighbourhood team or act as its accountable body.

It might even be the case, mightn't it, that the local association of traders says, "Our High Street will thrive if the back street also thrives. So, we'll volunteer to market the new image of the neighbourhood and help the local school and housing association to advertise and fill its vacant posts. Further, just as most town centres now have a centre manager, our neighbourhoods also needs a manager. We'll provide and fund one." Thus, there is no need at all for the Neighbourhood's Manager to emerge every time and everywhere from the public sector. They might be recruited either from the private or the voluntary one. There is no harm at all in injecting the attitudes and experiences of the private sector into the reformed public one.

Will all social services in all neighbourhoods be managed by one or other of the above in a set way? There is no one-size-fits-all alternative. Different combinations of the above will arise in different neighbourhoods.

So, in some neighbourhoods, most if not all services may be delivered by devolved parts of the public sector via the neighbourhood management team. In others, a successful school might undertake the duty of maintaining the local park and swimming pool. In others, a Housing Association or TMO might do so. In yet others, a strong neighbourhood forum or voluntary organisation might assume a leading role and maintain most local services. It's a case of horses for courses. In any one neighbourhood the key questions for residents to ask is: "Which agency is best placed to deliver which service?" and "Can we and the local authority regulate and inspect that service?"

That's the point of localism and self-determination. People in different neighbourhoods will make different choices. Diversity is inevitable. It works in those neighbourhoods which have tried it. We know that uniformity does not work in the many neighbourhoods which have suffered under it for several generations. So, let's go with what works and jettison a 150-year-old theory which does not work.

Before some centralising collectivist cries that this privatisation, it is necessary to remind them that it is the very opposite of privatisation. When we privatised an industry we took it out of collective state control and gave it to a private sector business to manage and run at a financial profit. The customer then either enabled it to succeed because they bought the product, or they closed it down because they chose to shop elsewhere.

The proposal localisation of services places the management of them in the hands of groups of ordinary local people whose task is to help each other to improve the delivery of the product. This is mutualism and neighbourly self-help. It takes us back to the eighteen hundreds before we reneged on the principle of subsidiary and turned down the cul-de-sac which lead from local self-help to remote central control.

Further, the neighbourhood plan which sets targets for the improvement of each service is worked out, implemented and reviewed by a combination of the residents forum and the locally accountable Neighbourhood Team. That is, mutualism is far more locally accountable and flexible than central planning.

There are three major prizes to be won by changing radically and localising the way many services are delivered. The first is that the quality of these services and life for millions of people will improve dramatically in the neighbourhoods where they live.

The second is that the political process will gain credibility because ordinary people will be able to (a) see that it can make a difference to their lives and (b) that they can influence it and be part of it. As the yawning credibility gap shrinks and is bridged it is, therefore, likely that the number of people who vote in local and national elections will increase. Indeed, increasing the number of people who vote from 20% to 50% in local elections should become a target and test of successful renewal.

The third is that we thereby necessarily change the 150 years old way we thinking about how to care for each other from being impersonal and remote to being personal and close at hand. Thus, we will change the way we act. It will make us behave better towards each other, to want to give as well as to receive. It will make not just better policies but it will make us better people.

We can see that, after very many years of trying and failing, neither the privatisation of conservatism nor the collectivism of socialism are appropriate ways of generating civil renewal. There is a different, a third, way. We are at the beginning of the process of understanding what that is and why it is vital that we supersede the failed attempt to impose socialism's second way or apply the private sector's first way to the social realm. It has its own, hitherto untapped, logic and generative power which, if unleashed, can change the way the political parties think and frame polices. In adding participatory to representative democracy it can breathe fresh life into the political process. It takes us from the Welfare State to the Welfare Society.

Collectivism and Individualism

Hitherto, a false distinction has been drawn between the collectivism of socialism and the individualism of Conservatism. It is important to stress that while these concepts have been taken up over the last hundred plus years by different philosophers and political parties, as if one was right and the other wrong, they are in fact the inseparable, mutually dependent, flip sides of the same social coin.

The Cathedral of civilization is the cumulative collective work of many, many, individual people toiling over many generations. The north wing is not independent. It can't stand on its own. It is not complete until the arched roof of the sun-facing East connects it to the West Wing.

Yet, collectivism became separated by philosophers into one distinct way of seeing the world, which was set against the allegedly opposed confines of choice and individualism. It is important to recognize that, in the practical reality of life, they are not separate but integral, interconnecting, parts of a wider, more exciting, ebb and flow of the whole.

The collectivism of Figure 25a (the sociological and socialist consensus) and the unrestrained individualism of Figure 25c (laissez-faire) are polar extremes which derive from the respective partial views of working class labour and property owning conservative. The maypole-like Figure 25b (the radical alternative) represents a blend of the two extremes which corresponds both to the way successful modern businesses are organised and to the new self-governing communities we describe. It highlights both the role of the individual the local agency and the social context in which individualism is expressed. It suggests a partnership rather than polar opposites, harmony rather than conflict. Except for those who do not believe there is such a thing as in 'society', the unadulterated individualism of Figure 25c is self evidently not applicable even to many economic aspects of human affairs or its risks doing the same sort of damage to reality as the imposition of Marx's collectivist theories have done. So, it is sensible to compare and contrast the pyramid-like collectivism in Figure 25a, which Marx, sociologists and the industrial world imposed on the human world, with Figure 25b, the maypole, which seems to bear the closest resemblance to the emerging reality of social relations in post-industrial society.

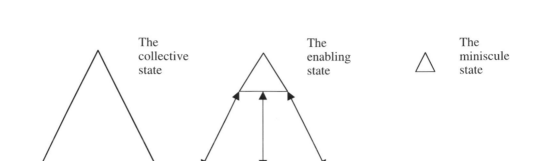

Figure 25: the first, second and third ways of picturing society.

Perhaps it should be stressed that pyramid-like organisations make it difficult for the environment, charity, value, the urban village and the character of man to thrive. Maypole-like ones stimulate them by refocusing government and creating an enabling state. The enduring, traditional qualities of life are heightened by the radical alternative of the maypole. These include wisdom, humour, spirit will and vision. They result in choice and rich diversity. The theoreticians of collectivism hardly recognize these characteristics. They are omitted from their analysis, explanations of and policies for society. The radical alternative gives them pride of place. They are irreducible entities – the catalytic spark of life without which neither explanation nor policy can be complete.

Whole societies and organisations within them do not just fit one or other typical pyramid – or maypole-like model. As Handy and Stewart point out, maypole-like organisations can easily become routinized and come to resemble pyramid-like ones, as has happened to the once-radical institutions of industrial society. These can survive for a while, but they will either disintegrate or go through a process of reform until they come to resemble the maypole.

Britain, other Western societies and organisations within them are at the moment in the painful process of transition from being pyramid-like to becoming maypole-like. While some within these societies still look to the past through the collectivist's eyes, others increasingly seek to accelerate the dawning of a new, post-industrial, era.

Collectivism	Blend of individualism and collective
Tradition, the family and local institutions are diminished.	Tradition, the family and local institutions are upheld.
The organisations' system of rules dominates the individual.	The individual is able to stay in control of events.
Initiative is stifled.	The individual is stretched.
Innovation is rare.	Innovation is the rule.
Development is feared.	Development is encouraged.
There is a rigid hierarchy of authority and no scope for change. The lower ranks can only challenge this authority by rebelling or leaving the system,	There is a natural hierarchy of talents and functions with plenty of scope for change. The individual and collective are reconciled through participation.
Rigidity encourages disrespect, especially from the lower ranks whose talents are unrecognised. This leads to conflict,	Flexibility encourages respect. There is a natural harmony or balance in social relations.
There are no leaders. Individualism and variety are discouraged. It is the rules of office not the individual which are respected.	Charismatic leaders are at a premium. Individualism and variety are encouraged. The office rules can be bent and re-created to get things done
The individual feels lost and isolated within a machine-like system.	The individual identifies with the community and organisation and gains fulfilment through them.
People are dependent. The 'system' binds people together.	People are self-reliant. Values bind people together.

Figure 26: A comparison of the values of collectivism versus a combination of individualism and collectivism.

The development of a theory which combines the virtues of both collectivist and individualistic ways of organising social affairs could mark the end of a period of major debate and conflict between those who argued for a caring public state and those who have advocated private initiative.

As post-industrial society emerges from the cocoon of constraint, we must accept that for too long it has been supposed that only the well-educated 20 per cent of the population, the confident, ambitious and affluent, are competent to run their own independent institutions, look after their own houses, use private health care and private schools and run their own businesses. Similarly, for too long, it has been assumed that the poorly educated 80 per cent of the population were so incompetent and dependent that they could only be housed, made healthy and educated within one-size-fits-all institutions which the State provided for them and that they could do none of these things for themselves.

It is no longer necessary to use dated supposition and theories to form a policy, which holds back the independent few in a vain, socially unbalancing, attempt to make them equal to the dependent majority and to uphold this act as if it were a caring virtue. Rather, the time has come when the natural privileges of independence and autonomy, which the ambitious were bold enough to forge for themselves, should be ungrudgingly offered to the many through the radical redefinition of the aims and functions of the State and the role of local government.

Sir Ralf Dahrendorf made the point well when he said that in future 'individuals will have to appreciate that philanthropy is a social obligation; companies will have to understand that it is in their enlightened self-interest' to give and to be involved in the life of the community in which they are situated. Above all, said Sir Ralf, 'we need a pact between Government and the voluntary sector which preserves all the sensitivity and flexibility of private action, but involves a major share of government funding.' The neighbourhood's use of its own budget and the entrepreneurial functions of the capacity builder and civic entrepreneur illustrate that 'government funding' does not mean 'grant' aid or the 'redistribution' of wealth but the use of finance to invest in the organisation of society in quite different, new, ways.

So, the third way is not a compromise between the extremes of left and right. It aims to blend the best of these worlds together. In so doing, it aims to include the third force of active citizens in the management of their own lives in the neighbourhoods where they live and raise their families. It proposes a new, powerful, alliance between citizens, the enabling state and the regulated market.

The principles behind this way and the reforms it implies can be summarised as follows:

1. We now know that in order to deliver welfare services we do not need to increase taxation, as the collectivist would have us do, nor do we need to lower taxes, as the individualist suggests. Rather, it is important to use existing money in quite different ways. It is vital that the taxpayer is able to see where their money is going – not on unproductive state bureaucracies, but to needy individuals and locally managed agencies which can use that money to good purpose. It is essential that local people gain a sense of ownership over taxpayer funded services so that they become local social assets through which welfare is delivered. Thus, the givers, the administrators and the receivers are connected in a transparent way, can identify with each other and recognize the role which each plays.

2. For most of the last century of the last millennium the Labour Party wanted to nationalise communal or social as well as economic endeavour. But, it only succeeded in stifling it, whilst the right have sought to privatise it and unintentionally ignored all those people who cannot stand on their own feet without mutual support and encouragement. Neither nationalization nor privatisation can unlock the social potential of excluded people or those who wish to assist them.

3. Self- belief, skills and power cannot be redistributed and given to people who do not have them. Nor, once lost, can they be regained over night. People have to build these virtues for themselves by associating with each other and constructing a new social hinterland. Replenishing eroded social capital is hard work and takes as much time as the greening of the desert.

4. It follows that the size and scope of the government should neither increase nor diminish. It is the nature of it which should change. It should develop a fresh enabling role, facilitate and not provide. It must develop from being a purely representative democracy in which people can only vote once a year for others to represent them to also being a participatory democracy in which people themselves are directly involved in shaping their own lives every day of the week.

It has been said that representative democracy is accountable. In the formal sense, it is. But, participatory democracy holds people to account for one another close at home where opinion, criticism and response can have immediate and telling effect. For example, a school is much more accountable if it has to justify the way it spends its budget to parents and local businesses in its own catchment area than when its budget can not be distinguished from those of all other schools. The same is true of the housing estate, health centre, police station, Community Development Trust and neighbourhood.

5. Once participatory democracy and the governance by people of their own neighbourhoods becomes the order of the day, then conventional party politics becomes largely redundant, especially at the local level. Most people are not concerned with political theory but with more practical matters. Is there litter in my street and, if so, how do I get it moved? Are my child and my neighbour frightened to go out at night and, if so, how can I help them to feel safer? Etc, etc. These are practical, every day all party and non-party questions, which require answers which are not prejudiced by theory or political caucuses.

6. We have to conclude that collectivists have committed their ultimate error in supposing that because the poor do not have power or wealth then they must organise themselves politically and take them from those who do have them. It follows from this assumption that rival parties – one for the poor and one for the rich – must lock horns in a class war which one might win eventually and the other might lose.

It is increasingly difficult to grasp that anyone can ever have supposed that the route to social progress was via conflict and victory or loss by one or another 'side' in work between workers and management and in politics between the poor and the rich, the haves and have-nots. But, they did and influential politicians still do. Lord Hattersley was still insisting, recently, that "the call for consensus is wrong" and that to determine issues "on their merit" is "dangerous for socialism." Yet, it is clear to most people that we must play to each other's strengths, not attack each other's weaknesses or accentuate our capacity to distrust and beat each other. Bringing the different sections of a community and the wider society into mutually productive alignment is not a "compromise" but an energizing and liberating virtue. Indeed, bringing different interest groups together does more than create a simple sum of them. It gives added value. It creates communal bonds and mutual understanding which tie people together and generates fresh energy, growth, 'flair' and 'flow'. In helping others rather than vying with them, we help ourselves and multiply rather than redistribute scarce resources.

7. It follows that just as the bankrupt mill and mine of the industrial era must close and be superseded, so also the theories which justified the failing services of the industrially derived Welfare State must be closed down and reopened in fresh guise to suit a new purpose.

Too often in the past politicians have supposed that they know best and that ordinary people, especially those in the most difficult areas in the country, can't play any part in their own solution. We now know that this no longer holds true, if it ever did.

Ordinary people know rather more than politicians about what is right for them and their neighbourhoods. With the careful encouragement which a new breed of Capacity Builder and Civic Entrepreneur can give, local people and local businesses hold many of the answers to questions which have bedevilled us for 100 years. It is now clear that the role of local and central government is not to impose solutions but to devise policies which enable more local solutions.

8. Many of the assumptions and political dichotomies of the twentieth century seem destined to fade as a fresh and radical alternative emerges, a third way which entails using neither the public nor the private sectors alone to deliver services. The woefully weakened "third" or "community" sector can, if strengthened, play a vital role – which also changes the black and white way we view the public and private sectors. The community sector can rejuvenate civil society close to home, where most people find their identity, well-being and purpose in life.

The advantage is clear. The third sector embodies mutual responsibility which is rooted in local neighbourhoods. It promotes a powerful sense of personal ownership, generates ethical investment, creates civic assets and local pride. It enhances and develops democracy by adding the quality of personal and communal participation to that of simple representation. It builds the capacity of ordinary people to shape and improve the quality of their lives, almost imperceptibly moving to a situation where the state no longer dominates but enables others in the private and third sectors to provide for themselves. It re-introduces tax-givers to the agencies and people they fund. It creates mutual appreciation, inclusion and the harmony of one society.

9. If free people are to live together in harmony and not conflict and support each other in sickness and in health, then once scorned overarching common values and a set of traditions which summarise and teach them become a common sense and practical necessity. Reinventing a culture which upholds these vital guides to choice and judgment will take time. Greening the a-cultural, overly rational, desert which has been bleaching social ground for so long is a huge undertaking. It will require changes as profound as those introduced by the Enlightenment and is far beyond the scope of any government, party or section of society.

These developments are progress not privatisation, liberation not competition. They change they very nature of government and entail a new compact or covenant between the people and local and central government.

This covenant is about to be invited onto the centre of the stage by a range of voices calling from the Four Corners of the land. They can be heard in Bromley by Bow, Birkenhead, Toxteth, Easterhouse, and Balsall Heath. For some time, these voices were hesitant and spoke in whispers. Then, they became an audible buzz. Today, the sound they make has risen to become a clarion call to unite the nation and propel us through the first decades of the new Millennium.

Can the most senior politicians, clerics and opinion leaders hear this call? Will they respond to it and give the people who voice it the authoritative lead they yearn for?

Chapter Eleven

CONCLUSION & RECOMMENDATIONS

We know the following:

- An out of control child whose parent(s) lack child rearing skills because the shrinking family no longer transmits these can be controlled within days when the parent(s) are shown by experienced parents how to use praise and sanctions properly and assert their authority effectively.
- A failing business can be turned into a success if new management treats the customer with respect and provides them with the product they desire.
- A failing school can be turned round if the head who has lost control of it is either removed or helped by a successful head who knows how to command the respect of the teachers and other staff, pupils and parents and helps them to plan ahead to achieve the best results.

We also now know – because it has too been done – that even the most squalid neighbourhood can be turned by residents into a confident one in which people are proud to live. All that is needed for this to happen is for the following ingredients to be brought into productive alignment:

- The poor quality of life is recognised and it is accepted that it could be greatly improved.
- A number of Active Citizens who wish to make a difference are identified and supported.
- Their Capacity to work with their neighbours is encouraged so that they can build local networks, voluntary organisations and a strong community.
- These Active Citizens and the community are able to work with statutory service suppliers, hold them to account so their services improve and/or are supplied and managed locally.
- A Neighbourhood Plan is agreed and implemented with the help of a Neighbourhood Strategic Partnership and a local budget derived from mainstream funding.

- Leadership is shown and a communal authority is constructed which results in a previously disorganised, under performing, set of residents and professionals playing to each others strong points.
- The local authority and government are sympathetic, help and enable the new local partnerships to function smoothly.

This recipe for success is easily put into words. But, hitherto, it has been difficult to deliver in practice.

How quickly can the Roger Bannisters of the race to renew civil society show 3,000 other runners in 3,000 other neighbourhoods that it is worth their while to persist and not collapse panting at the starting line because they do not believe they have the stamina to reach the finishing tape?

Breaking the 4 minute mile of renewal took an almost super-human effort by those few social entrepreneurs in the few neighbourhoods which, to date, have become renewed. The scale of this effort risks deterring the 3,000 others needed to run the race in their excluded neighbourhood. So, this book shows them why, in future, with training and resources, a supporting culture and enabling authority the race can be run by ordinary mortals every day of the year. Thus, it is vital that politicians, civil servants, local government officials and would-be active citizens, note its advice.

Triggering the series of rolling programmes of neighbourhood renewal described above is relatively easy – given the recognition and the development of the political will needed to fully support what is already beginning to happen naturally.

Yet, "there are none so deaf as those who will not hear or blind as those who will not see."

For at least 50 years, if not, since the Enlightenment, the social bonds which tie us together in mutual love and support have been fraying. Aspects of this have been beneficial. The social bonds of yester-year were too tight and constraining. It is good that they have become looser, more flexible and tolerant of diversity. But the pendulum has swung too far in the opposite direction and the "me, mine, I want it now" culture of permissiveness and license has snapped the bonds which tied us together in mutual support. This has caused too many of us to fail to care for each other, most noticeably in our inner and outer city neighbourhoods. It has made life for very many people far more miserable, and fearful than successive policy makers and metropolitan sophisticates can imagine.

It must be all the harder to listen to the voice of ordinary people when the message they articulate is that the caring policy maker and politician and the welfare state they created to do good to ordinary folk has contributed to this problem. How ungrateful can people be? How can so many politicians, policy makers and commentators have got it wrong for so long? Surely the customer is wrong, not the policy?

However, the once still small voice of anguish has not gone away. On the contrary, with the years, it has grown louder and louder. It now fills the surgeries of Councillors and M.P's every Friday. It screams at us from the front pages of the press as one more elderly lady is mugged by one more sixteen year old boy and as Damilola Taylor dies in that bleak stairwell in Peckham. Yet, as the politician still appears deaf even to a shout, fewer and fewer people vote as they cry: "Help. Life in our neighbourhood is hell. We are afraid to go out at night. We dare not let our children play outside their own front door. What are you going to do? Something must be done!"

The Welfare State's sophisticated one-size-fits-all services of housing, environment, health, education and neighbourhood governance are not working. Simply throwing more money at them won't work either. For, current practices do not take into account the local voice, local intelligence, local enterprise. To turn so many neighbourhoods from failure to success will not be easy. But, at least, politicians and policy makers have now heard the voice of the masses distilled through the agonised cries of Damilola Taylor, James Bulger and others. And, they acknowledge that the Bottom-up efforts of some residents and professionals in some neighbourhoods like Balsall Heath and Castle Vale are working. They imply a radically different approach to renewal and the creation of a Welfare Society. A social and political tipping point is at hand. The tide really is turning.

A series regional debates and a national conversation

The tide will turn faster if we can accept the following:

- Everyone, especially children, needs a strong family, neighbourly and communal bonds which give them an identity and the mutual ability to sustain a good quality of life.
- For various reasons – globalism, technology, top-down planning – we have taken more out of civil society than we have put into it. So, we are no longer able to sustain those bonds and the good life. This affects the affluent who are materially rich but spiritually poor and the materially poor who lack the spiritual strength to make a difference.
- That is, there now is a hole in the 'social ozone layer' as surely as we discovered there was one in the physical ozone layer. The cathedral of civilisation crumbles and is ill maintained. In order to convey these truths to most people, we need an all-party-and-none debate about the hole in the social ozone layer and how to fill it. We need that debate nationally and we need it locally so that we all come to hear and see the scale of the problem and the nature of a solution.

The Active Citizen

People live and find their identity in neighbourhoods. There are 3,000+ excluded neighbourhoods which suffer from multiple deprivation and as many more, which suffer from social deprivation but not other forms of deprivation.

Yet, in every neighbourhood there is a can-doer, a Gloria who knows what they want for themselves and their neighbours but lack the resources, including the confidence, to achieve it.

Active Citizens may just wish to help their own and other families or to empower the whole community. There are many forms of activity they may wish to engage in. All need to be resourced and supported by a new 'Culture of Caring' which is reinforced by these activities:

- Just as we have a Remembrance Day, so we need a Care in the Community Day in which the whole nation is invited to participate.
- On that day, schools and communities should be asked to induct every cohort of 18 year olds into adult citizenship – not just Asylum seekers.
- In the style of a 'gap year' or National Service we need a voluntary 'Care in the Community' year in which young people are asked to choose one of a number of activities from which they can graduate with a special certificate.
- Incentives to take this gap year of care, in which the hole in the social ozone layer is filled, might include a graduation certificate which qualifies the recipient to a 50% discount on their student debt or a citizen's wage for these who have left full-time study.
- Active Citizens need to be resourced, supported and their action coordinated and broadcast. They are today's priests. Their networks are today's broad church. They are the bricks and mortar of the social cathedral.

The empowered neighbourhood

The over centralised, top-down, one-size-fits-all services have been supplied 'for' people, not with them. The existing lines of governance have cut people up. They have not pulled them up.

So, those Active Citizens who wish to empower their neighbourhood, reduce crime, improve the environment, make people healthier, create a good neighbourhood image of which people can be proud, face many obstacles and need every support to overcome them. In particular, they need:

- Capacity Building staff and resources.
- A single pot which they can access for capacity building funds.
- Help from BitC and a Trades Union in the Community (TuitC)
- Training and buddy schemes.

- The ability to access mainstream budgets and to have these budgets disentangled from far wider ones so that they become targeted on neighbourhoods and can be accounted for.
- Neighbourhood Management and a Neighbourhood Manager as well as a neighbourhood budget.
- A Neighbourhood Forum, perhaps, but not necessarily, a Parish Council.

The vast 'top-down' renewal sums granted by ODPM and other ministries need to be refocused to generate capacity building, neighbourhood management and drive the civil renewal debate, policy and practice.

If resourced and encouraged, the few success stories can lead a series of regional Rolling Programmes of Flourishing Neighbourhoods. Having recovered, Gloria is the best mentor and catalyst for the disempowered Gloria's in other neighbourhoods. Guide neighbourhoods can help weaker ones until all are en-route to recovery. These rolling programmes need to be organised locally and nationally with will, gusto, and determination or ordinary folk will stumble.

Local Authorities and Police, PCTs etc

We need Local Authorities more than ever, but not as industrial-age 'doers' and 'providers' of services, more as 'enablers' and 'conductors of an orchestra' of service suppliers which includes third sector and neighbourhood suppliers. This gives LA's a positive, strategic, empowering role and opens the door to increased levels of appreciation and voting.

This is exciting, but many LA's and other statutory agencies will feel threatened. So:

- It's no good expecting them to reform voluntarily. They must be made to do it.
- As with schools when they became Locally Managed, they must be shown how to do it and given training, time scales to meet and models which show them what they are aiming to achieve.
- Just as there is good Active Citizen and Empowered Neighbourhood practice, so there are bits and pieces of good L.A, Police etc practice. We need to put the different bits and pieces together in a treasure trail or jigsaw puzzle of good practice so the doubters can see that it works.

A bottom-up and top-down partnership

Neither civil nor civic society can exist in isolation. As a more robust civil society is built by active citizens, capacity builders and participatory democracy, so civic society needs to make space for it and change from 'doing' to 'enabling' mode. Thus, a bold, dynamic, new partnership between them is emerging. So far, only bits and pieces of the jig saw puzzle of this new way of picturing society are available.

But, enough is in place in Wolverhampton, Bradford, Liverpool, Birmingham and other urban areas for us to glimpse the future. We need to forge a new compact between the individual and the state. Indeed, wherever we look, in place of an overbearing Welfare State is emerging a new kind of Welfare Society.

The eventual outcome spells a very different way of governing and caring for ourselves in the first century of the third, new, Millennium than developed in the last century of the second Millennium. These are exciting, vitally important times for the evolving Cathedral.

The assertion of a moral code and authority

Street stewards, capacity builders, and Neighbourhood Managers need the help of all the parties and all the faiths to assert a common set of standards which can guide them with authority and conviction through difficult times and remind everyone of their obligations and duties.

We need to double the vote in local elections and increase it in general ones by showing that participatory democracy can restore some point and purpose to the representative kind. We need to elect representatives we can trust and then we need to maintain that trust in them, even when we disagree with them.

If this is to happen, politicians of both the left and right will have to rethink their political ideology from which they derive their manifesto. They need to listen to the still, small, voice of ordinary folk and consider the needs of the whole of a neighbourhood and society, not just one bit of it.

Even ten years ago, the debate and the action needed to transform so many desolate neighbourhoods seemed distant. Then, Gloria's voice cried in the wilderness and survival, let alone success, seemed to be light years away. Then, she could not sell her house or let her children play in the garden, let alone in the street

Today, the transformation of Castle Vale, Balsall Heath and a handful of other neighbourhoods has helped us to see how the process of recovery can be speeded.

Government alone can't do this. Without the help of others, it can set a lead, resource and drive the proposed policy and strategy. The debate has to be engaged by all the parties, all the faiths and all sectors and to last as long as the one about stewarding the environment to mend the hole in the physical ozone layer.

In Birmingham, the debate has already started. A series of lectures and seminars are underway with the title: "Civil Renewal: The Chamberlain lectures." Birmingham is also linking top and bottom, public and community in a combined attempt to create an array of Flourishing Neighbourhoods or Urban Villages as a kind of practical implementation of the debate.

Wolverhampton is even more advanced. So, it is clear that other Towns and Cities can feed into and gain from the proposed national debate. A year or so after this book is published an edited version of the Chamberlain Lectures and the debate they precipitate will be published. It will contain the contributions of David Blunkett, David Willets, Oliver Letwin, the Bishop of Birmingham, the Chief Constable of the West Midlands, Gloria Dillion and her friend Naseem Akhtar and the views of two hundred critical participants. It will take the debate beyond the limitations of this book and challenge others to join it and take it further.

The time is ripe. Many people are ready to play their part. But, if ordinary folk are to make headway, they really do need the support and encouragement of the leaders of all the parties, all the faiths and of entrepreneurs within the private sector. Can they muster the will? Can they see the point of a stitch in time now to avoid the disaster of having to make nine tomorrow? Can they repair the tattered fabric, the hole, in the social ozone layer?

If our children and children's children are to inherit a robust Cathedral and a spirited quality of life, the answer to these questions has to be not whether but when and how soon.

INDEX

BIBLIOGRAPHY

Ashdown, Paddy, *Beyond Westminster*, Simon and Schuster
Atkinson, Dick, *Radical Alternative, Orthodox Consensus*, Heineman
Atkinson, Dick, *Radical Urban Solutions*, Heineman
Atkinson, Dick, *Cities of Pride*, Heineman
Atkinson, Dick, *The Common Sense of Community*, DEMOS
Atkinson, Dick, *Towards Self-governing Schools*, IEA
Atkinson, Dick, *Urban Renaissance*, Brewin Books
Attwood, Chris, *2001 Home Office Citizenship Survey*, Home Office
Baker, Nicola, *Building a Relational Society*, Arena
Bright, Jon, *Turning the Tide*, DEMOS
Canterbury, Archbishop of, *Faith in the City*, Church House
Christie, Ian, *An Inclusive Future*, DEMOS
Csikszentmihalyi, Mihaly, *Living Well*, Weidenfeld and Nicolson
Darling, Alastair, *The Changing Welfare State*, HMSO
Davies, Nick, *Dark Heart*, Vintage
Elstee, John, *Local Justice*, Cambridge Press
Etzioni, Amitai, *The Spirit of Community*, Crown
Field, Frank, *Making Welfare Work*, Institute of Community Studies
Fordham, Scott, Kemp, Richard and Croswley, Paul, *Going the extra mile*, The JRF
Gidens, Anthony, *The Third Way*, Polity
Golman, Daniel, *Emotional Intelligence*, Bloomsbury
Handy, Charles, *The Age of Unreason*, Hutchinson
Holman, Robert, *A New Deal for Social Welfare*, Lion
Leadbeater Charles, *The Rise of the Social Entrepreneur*, DEMOS
Leadbeater, Charles and Gross, Sue, *Civic Entrepreneur*, DEMOS
Leadbeater, Charles, *Living on Thin Air*, Viking
Mujtaba & Lari, *Western Civilisation Through Muslim Eyes*, Panjtani Books
Olasky, Marvin, *Compassionate Conservation*, Free Press
Osborne and Gaebler, *Reinventing Government*, Addison Wesley and Renguine
Philips, Melanic, *All shall have Prizes*, Little Brown
Power, Anne & Tunstall, *Dangerous Disorder*, The Joseph Rowntree Foundation
Power, Anne & Mumford, Katherine, *The Slow Death of Great Cities*
Power, Anne, *Estates of the Edge*, Macmillan Press
Power, Anne, *One Size does not fit All*, BCC
Putnam, Robert, *Bowling Alone*, Simon and Schuster

Rifkin, Jeremy, *The End of Work*, Tarcher Puntnan
Rodgers, Lord Richard, *Towards Urban Renaissance*, HMSO
Shumacher, Eric, *Small is Beautiful*, Penguin
Sacks, Johnathon, *Faith in the Future*, Darton, Longman & Treld
Sacks, Johnathon, *The Politics of Hope*, Jonathan Cape
Skidelsky, Robert, *Beyond the Welfare State*, Social Market Foundation
Stewart, Valarie, *The David Solution*, Gower
Taylor, Marilyn, *Top Down meets Bottom Up*, The Joseph Rowntree Foundation
Taylor, Marilyn, *Unleashing the Potential*, The Joseph Rowntree Foundation
Thake, Stephen, *Staying the course*
Thake, Stephen, *Practical People, Noble Causes*, The JRF
Van der Eyben, Williams, *Home-start*, Home-start consultancy
Wadhams, Chris, *Thursday's Children*, The Quest Trust
Wales, The Prince of, *A Vision of Britain*, Doubleday
Wann, Mai, *Building Social Capital*, IPPR
Willets, David, *Civic Conservatism*, The Social Market Foundation
Willets, David, *Modern Conservatism*, Penguin Books
Wilson, James Q, *The Moral Sense*, Free Press
Whelan, Robert, *Involuntary Action*, IEA
Whelan, Robert, *Octavia Hill*, IEA